AN INTRODUCTION

TO THE

HISTORY OF THE SCIENCE OF POLITICS

Sir Frederick Pollock (1845-1937) was educated at Eton and Cambridge, and was admitted to the bar in 1871. He was professor of jurisprudence at University College, London (1882-1883) and at Oxford University (1883-1903). He served as editor of the *Law Quarterly Review* from 1885 until 1919 and as editor-in-chief of the *Law Reports* from 1895 to 1935. In 1914, he was appointed judge of the Cinque Ports admiralty court. Among his publications are *Principles of Contract* (1876), *Spinoza* (1880), *The Land Laws* (1882), and, with F. W. Maitland, *The History of English Law* (1895).

AN INTRODUCTION TO THE

HISTORY

OF THE

SCIENCE OF POLITICS

By Frederick Pollock

Beacon Press   Beacon Hill   Boston

To the Memory

OF

LORD ACTON

FOREWORD

THIS Essay, delivered as a course of lectures at the Royal Institution in 1882, and shortly afterwards published as a series of articles in the *Fortnightly Review*, was issued in its present shape in 1890. Since that time there have been several reissues with slight corrections and additions; and the book has been found useful enough in foreign countries to be translated into French (*Introduction à l'étude de la science politique*, etc., Paris, 1893), German (*Kurze Geschichte der Staatslehre*, Leipzig, in Reclam's Universal-Bibliothek, 1893), and Polish (1902); I have also heard of but not seen an unauthorized Russian version. After twenty years a more thorough revision seems called for. I have expressed my own views with more freedom in several places, increased the number of references in the notes, and added to them some indications of the points which I might develop if I ever had time to enlarge this outline. Great part of the last chapter has been rewritten, with the result, I hope, of making it better, and, I am sure, of making it at least more coherent.

The modern fashion of a bibliographical list of authorities is inapplicable to so small a book; I may mention, however, that a good one down to 1902 is appended to W. A. Dunning's *History of Political Theories, Ancient and Mediœval*.

In the present re-issue some critical and bibliographical additions have been made to the notes. The internal controversies of Socialism in its many varieties (p. 133) have been aggravated by the war still raging; and we have learnt that, although most Socialists profess anti-militarist principles, the political mechanism of modern war is essentially socialist.

F. P.

May 1918.

CONTENTS

I.—THE BEGINNINGS OF POLITICAL SCIENCE

	PAGE
The place of Politics among the Sciences	2
Division of Sciences	4
Speculative and Practical Departments of Moral Science	6
Field of Political Science	8
Ideal of Political Life in Ancient Athens	10
Rudiments of Political Theory in our reports of Socrates	12
Plato's Developments	13
His Republic Ideal, not Practical	14
New Departure of Aristotle; his Practical Method	15
Aristotle's "Politics"	17
Aristotle's "Natural Citizenship" and Rousseau's "Social Contract"	18
Economical Teaching of Aristotle	21
His Criticisms of Plato's Communism	22
The Citizen and the City defined	24
Good and Bad Constitutions	26
Aristotle's Views of Citizenship applied to the Modern State	27

PAGE

DECAY OF POLITICAL SCIENCE IN GREECE AFTER THE ROMAN
CONQUEST 30

CICERO'S PHILOSOPHICAL WORKS 32

II.—THE MIDDLE AGES AND THE RENAISSANCE

STRUGGLE BETWEEN THE EMPEROR FREDERICK II. AND THE
PAPACY 35

ST. THOMAS AQUINAS "DE REGIMINE PRINCIPUM," AND
DANTE "DE MONARCHIA" 37

DANTE'S IDEAL MONARCH 40

WRITERS ON POLITICS BEFORE MACHIAVELLI . . . 41

POLITICAL PRINCIPLES OF MACHIAVELLI . . . 43

HIS SCHEME FOR THE RESTORATION OF ITALIAN UNITY . 45

BODIN'S TREATISE "OF COMMONWEALTH" . . . 47

HIS CONCEPTION OF SOVEREIGNTY 48

MORAL AND GENERAL LIMITATIONS OF SOVEREIGN POWER . 53

FORTESCUE ON THE ENGLISH MONARCHY, AND MORE'S
"UTOPIA" 56

SIR THOMAS SMITH ON THE OMNIPOTENCE OF PARLIAMENT . 57

HOBBES'S "LEVIATHAN" 59

ORIGIN OF CIVIL SOCIETY IN CONTRACT . . . 59

RELATIONS OF THE SOVEREIGN AND THE SUBJECT . . 61

DEFINITION OF RIGHT AND WRONG 65

SUBSEQUENT TREATMENT OF HOBBES'S DOCTRINES . . 67

III.—THE EIGHTEENTH CENTURY AND THE SOCIAL
CONTRACT

LOCKE ON CIVIL GOVERNMENT 69

THE STATE OF NATURE AND THE STATE OF WAR . . 71

PAGE

POLITICAL SOCIETY 72

AUTHORITY OF THE LEGISLATIVE POWER . . . 74

LEGALITY OF A CHANGE OF GOVERNMENT . . . 76

PREROGATIVE OF THE CROWN 79

ROUSSEAU AND THE *CONTRAT SOCIAL* . . . 79

THE SOVEREIGN PEOPLE 80

DECLARATION OF THE RIGHTS OF MAN . . . 84

BLACKSTONE ON LOCKE'S PRINCIPLES . . . 85

MONTESQUIEU'S *ESPRIT DES LOIS* . . . 87

HIS EXCELLENCIES AND FAULTS . . . 87

BURKE 90

EXPERIENCE *VERSUS* DOGMATISM . . . 90

WILL OF THE MAJORITY 93

PRINCIPLES OF 1789 95

EXPEDIENCY AND LEGALITY 96

IV.—MODERN THEORIES OF SOVEREIGNTY AND LEGISLATION

CLASSIFICATION OF THEORETICAL AND APPLIED POLITICS . 98

BENTHAM: HIS "FRAGMENT ON GOVERNMENT" . . 101

DEFINITION OF POLITICAL SOCIETY . . . 103

SOVEREIGNTY AND OBEDIENCE . . . 104

THE RULE OF UTILITY 106

AUSTIN 109

INSULARITY OF HIS DOCTRINE . . . 111

PRACTICAL SEAT OF POLITICAL SUPREMACY . . 114

THE CROWN AND THE ESTATES OF THE REALM . . 116

CONVENTIONS OF CONSTITUTIONAL PRACTICE . . 117

UTILITARIANS AND LAW OF NATURE . . . 118

	PAGE
CONTINENTAL PHILOSOPHY AND ENGLISH SCHOOL	122
THE HISTORICAL SCHOOL	126
MODERN DEVELOPMENTS	128
INDIVIDUALISM AND LIMITS OF STATE INTERFERENCE	130
HUMBOLDT, MILL, LABOULAYE	131
SPENCER, HUXLEY	132
SOCIALISM	133
CENTRALISED AND LOCAL REGULATION	133
BACK TO ARISTOTLE	134
INDEX (MAINLY OF PROPER NAMES)	137

I

THE BEGINNINGS OF POLITICAL SCIENCE—SCIENCE IN GREEK PHILOSOPHY

No good Brahman begins any literary work without a formula of salutation to Ganeśa, the elephant headed patron-god of learning. In the West we are not so punctilious about forms ; yet we might with some fitness open our undertakings in philosophy and science by saluting expressly or tacitly the memory of Aristotle. For, as Greece is to us the mother of almost everything that makes life worthy to be lived, so is Aristotle especially the father of science and scientific method ; and during the centuries when the lessons of Greece were forgotten, the name and work of Aristotle (used indeed in a manner and for purposes he would have marvelled at) were almost the only links that still bound the modern to the Hellenic world.

With regard to our present subject Aristotle's claim is evident and eminent. He has been recognised as the founder of political science by the general voice of posterity. There was political speculation before him, but it was he who first brought to bear on political phenomena the patient analysis and unbiassed research which are the proper marks and virtues of scientific inquiry. The science of politics, like so much else of our knowledge and endeavours to know, begins with Aristotle. In this as in other things his organising genius consolidated the scattered material of his predecessors, and left a compact structure. From Aristotle onwards we shall now try to follow the fortunes and growth of this science. It is not a tale of continuous and rapid advance like the history of the exact sciences, or even of those natural sciences in which mathematical precision is not attainable. On the contrary, we shall find much wild speculation, and many grave mistakes. But we shall also find a good deal of real advance, if we attend to what has been done by scientific inquirers rather than what has been put forward under the name of science by social and political agitation, and do not allow the failures to blind our eyes to the success.

Before we enter on the history it may be as well to take a rough general view of the place of the theory of politics in human knowledge. Many persons would perhaps deny that there is any science of politics at all. If they meant that there is no body of rules from which a Prime Minister may infallibly learn how to command a majority, they would be right as to the fact, but would betray a rather inadequate notion of what science is. There is a science of politics in the same sense, and to the same, or about the same, extent, as there is a science of morals. Whatever systematic moralists may have professed to think, it is at least doubtful whether systems of moral philosophy have been of much direct use in helping people to decide actual questions of conduct. For my own part, I would in a case of conscience rather consult a right-minded and sensible friend than any moral philosopher in the world. I should think neither the better nor the worse of his advice if he happened also to be a student of philosophy. Nevertheless few educated persons will refuse to admit that inquiry into the nature and origin of moral rules is legitimate and useful, or will maintain that the endeavour to refer them, historically or rationally, to general principles is altogether idle. Men, being moral beings, are led to reflect on the nature of right and wrong, and the functions of conscience ; being citizens, they are equally led to reflect on the nature of the State, the functions of government, and the origin and authority of civil duty. This latter inquiry is indeed more practical than the other ; for political theories of the most general kind often have considerable direct influence in public affairs, which cannot, I think, be said of ethical theories. The declaration of the Rights of Man by the French Constituent Assembly has certainly not been without practical effect. It consists of general statements of what men, as men, are entitled to and may justly demand. If true, the statements are of the utmost importance to politicians and legislators ; if false, they are highly mischievous. In either case they purport to be propositions of political science. M. Barthélemy St. Hilaire informed the world in 1848 that they were the crown and sum of all the political science of all former ages.   Claiming such authority, and having in fact influenced men's minds, the principles thus enounced cannot be merely disregarded; and it is scientific criticism that must establish or refute them.   To the persons who deny the necessity or possibility of philosophy it is a sufficient answer that at all events critical philosophy is needful for the exposure of philosophies falsely so called; and in the same way political science must and does exist, if it were only for the refutation of absurd political theories and projects.

To show how I conceive politics to fit into the general scheme of our knowledge, I adopt the old-fashioned division of the sciences into natural and moral.[1]   By this I do not mean to commit myself to any general

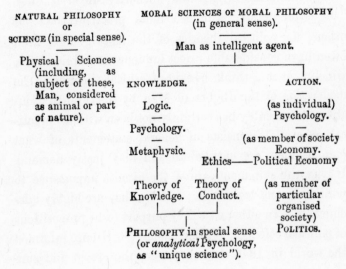

[1]   SCIENCE OR PHILOSOPHY (in widest sense).

NATURAL PHILOSOPHY or SCIENCE (in special sense).	MORAL SCIENCES or MORAL PHILOSOPHY (in general sense).
	Man as intelligent agent.

Physical   Sciences (including,   as subject of these, Man, considered as animal or part of nature).

KNOWLEDGE.   ACTION.
—   —
Logic.   (as individual)
—   Psychology.
Psychology.
—   (as member of society
Metaphysic.   Economy.
                Ethics——Political Economy
Theory of   Theory of   —
Knowledge.   Conduct.   (as member of
                particular
                organised
                society)
PHILOSOPHY in special sense   POLITICS.
(or *analytical* Psychology,
as "unique science").

doctrine. I do not see why there should be any one classification which is absolutely right in itself, or why we should not use different classifications for different purposes. From some points of view it may be proper to neglect entirely the distinction I now mean to use, as was done, for example, by Herbert Spencer in his essay on the classification of the sciences. In ultimate analysis the distinction may be made to vanish. At present I do not want to carry matters to ultimate analysis, but to regard the study of politics as belonging to a kind of inquiries which for ordinary practical purposes are sufficiently well marked off from others. In the natural sciences we have to do with the material world, and man's bodily organism as part thereof. In the moral sciences we have to do with man as intelligent, and to study the laws of his intelligent action. The general aim and method are the same—the discovery of truth by the reasoned investigation of facts ; but the means are widely different. In the natural sciences the work is done, broadly speaking, on phenomena present to the senses and with instruments of manual use. In the moral sciences the matter is present only in reflection, and the instruments are language and books. Hence there are wide differences in the manner of the student's work, the nature of the results, and the power of verifying them ; and these are worth marking, if only to perceive that the comparative inexactness of the moral sciences is not the fault of the men who have devoted their abilities to them, but depends, as Aristotle already saw, on the nature of their subject-matter. The sub-divisions of natural science do not now concern us. The moral sciences may be divided into speculative and practical branches. In the former we consider man as knowing and thinking; in the latter as feeling and acting. It is questionable, again, if this division will hold in final analysis. My own opinion is that it will not, or that knowledge and action are not really separable; but it corresponds to a difference sufficiently obvious in the common course of life. For the speculative branch, or the laws of thought, we have logic (whatever its exact place among or beside the speculative sciences ought to be) and metaphysic, which leads us to the all-devouring question of questions—what knowledge is, and how it is possible at all. Thus from the theory of knowledge on the speculative side, as also from ethics on the practical side, we are landed (or cast adrift might be thought by some the better phrase) on philosophy in the special sense, which is really apart from the sciences both moral and natural; for the organised knowledge of particular kinds of phenomena cannot include the analysis of knowledge itself. This I mention only by the way, to show that philosophy will not be exorcised by any ingenious arrangement of the sciences. She

¹ Not attempting a complete division, I purposely leave much open : as whether the pure sciences of space and number should stand at the head of the physical sciences, or be set apart by themselves, as not dealing with any one fact of nature, but fixing the general conditions of exact knowledge of the external world. Again, I offer no opinion about logic, save that it belongs to the speculative as distinct from the practical side of the moral sciences. There is a question (analogous to that of the pure sciences) whether it is a special science at all, and further and very difficult questions of its relation to psychology and metaphysics.

laughs at the pitchfork of Auguste Comte, and comes back at every turn, taking her revenge in a thousand ways on the blunders of popular thinking. Psychology belongs in a manner to both the speculative and the practical branch, being intimately connected alike with metaphysics and with ethics. On the practical side we may regard it as the study of man's action considered simply as an individual. But then we cannot be content with studying men as individuals. They live together in societies, and we know of no time when they did not. Hence the actions of man in society are the subject of a further kind of study, which is now commonly called Sociology. The word is offensive to scholars as being a barbarously formed hybrid;[1] and although it is too late to quarrel with anybody for using it, I should prefer Economy as a general name for the study of men's common life short of specific reference to the State. Such usage of the term corresponds pretty closely to Aristotle's. An important branch of this is what we all know as political economy, remarkable as the one department of the moral sciences which has assumed a semi-exact character. We must not be tempted to pursue the inquiry how far that character can in truth be justly ascribed to it. Another branch is ethics, if with the Greeks we regard ethics as dealing essentially with man in his relations to his fellow-men.

[1] If such a Latin word could exist at all, it could only mean a science of partnerships or alliances. One must not push these objections too far, however. Suicide, as was once pointed out at Cambridge by the opponent of a Latin thesis, "Recte statuit Paleius de suicidiis," could as a Latin word mean nothing but killing swine.

And indeed, whatever may be thought of the existence of absolute or purely self-regarding duties, or of the possibility of a moral sense arising otherwise than in society, it is undoubted that the great bulk of moral duties have regard to other persons. Without passing judgment on controverted questions, therefore, we may practically class ethics as a social science. Lastly, we come to consider man not only as a member of society, but as a member of some particular society, organised in a particular way, and exercising supreme authority over its members ; in other words, we consider man as a citizen, and the citizen in his relations to the State. Thus the field is indicated for the science of politics : a science dealing with matter so rich and various that from the beginning it has been embarrassed by this weight of wealth. Its sub-divisions will be more conveniently mentioned when we arrive at the period of its history in which they become distinct. At this point it is enough to say that the foundation and general constitution of the State, the forms and administration of government, and the principles and method of legislation seem naturally to fall asunder as heads under which the topics of political science may be grouped, though a strictly accurate and exclusive division is hardly possible ; and we must add as another head, more clearly marked off from all these, the consideration of the State as a single and complete unit of a higher order, capable of definite relations to other like units.

Aristotle, as we have said, is the founder of the science ; but not even the greatest of men can make a

science out of nothing, and a word of remembrance must
be given to the men and the conditions that made Aristotle's work possible.   There cannot be a theory of constitutions and statesmanship until civilised politics and
statesmen exist in fact, any more than there can be a
theory of ethics unless in a society which is already
moral.   Political speculation was suggested and invited
by the variety of political constitutions existing in
Greek cities, and most of all by the brilliant political
activity and resource displayed in the city of cities,
where in art, in letters, and in civil life the power and
beauty of Hellenic genius came to their full height ;
the city which our own Milton, an artist and Hellenist in
spite of his Puritanism, celebrated as the eye of Greece,[1]
and Swinburne, who had studied Greek poetry and
art as deeply as Milton, and more freely, sang of in
his *Erechtheus* in lines not unworthy of her own
tragedians—

"The fruitful immortal anointed adored
    Dear city of men without master or lord,
    Fair fortress and fostress of sons born free,
    Who stand in her sight and in thine, O sun,
    Slaves of no man, subjects of none ;
    A wonder enthroned on the hills and sea,
    A maiden crowned with a fourfold glory
    That none from the pride of her head may rend,
    Violet and olive-leaf purple and hoary,
    Song-wreath and story the fairest of fame,
    Flowers that the winter can blast not or bend :
    A light upon earth as the sun's own flame,
        A name as his name,
    Athens, a praise without end."

[1] True, it is by the mouth of Satan ; but Milton constantly neglects
the caution expressed at a later time about letting the devil have the
best tunes.

Pericles, the first of Athenian statesmen, was also one of the greatest statesmen who have ever lived. The speech delivered by him at the funeral of the Athenians who fell in the first campaign of the Peloponnesian war, and related by Thucydides, contains a description and an ideal of the state which, though sketched out in bold and broad lines and for popular effect, may help us to the knowledge of the soil that was ready for Plato and Aristotle to till. We cannot be sure, indeed, that Pericles actually spoke the words attributed to him by Thucydides ; but we may be sure, at the very least, that they are such as Thucydides thought Pericles likely to say, and an Athenian audience to approve ; and, considering the publicity and solemnity of the occasion, and the number of persons (Thucydides himself, in all probability, being among them) who must have preserved a vivid memory of what they heard, I am much disposed to think that we have in Thucydides a substantially correct account of what Pericles did say. What the student of politics has to note is this : there runs all through the speech the conception of the city, not as a mere dwelling-place or provision for material security, but as the sphere of man's higher activity. There is embodied in the city, in its laws, customs, and institutions, a pattern and ideal of life for the citizen. And the glory of Athens is that her ideal is better than others ; Athens has reached the highest pitch of civilisation yet attained, and is a school for all Hellas. She aims at producing a better type of man than other cities ; natural abilities being equal, man's faculties are more fully and variously developed at Athens than anywhere else. And this is effected, not by a pedantic and irksome course of training (after the fashion of the Lacedæmonian enemy),[1] but by the free and generous education of a refined life. "We aim," said Pericles, "at a life beautiful without extravagance, and contemplative without unmanliness; wealth is in our eyes a thing not for ostentation but for reasonable use; and it is not the acknowledgment of poverty we think disgraceful, but the want of endeavour to avoid it"—words from which our modern society still has much to learn. And it was this loftiness of aim, this appreciation of the worth of human life, which justified Athens in aiming likewise at primacy among the Greek states. If Pericles had used the jargon of modern diplomacy, he would have said that Athens had a mission to fulfil in holding up the best attainable exemplar of a civilised community. And therefore he bade the Athenians to quit themselves like men for a city dear to them by such titles, and to be strong in their father's renown and in their own courage, knowing that their renown too would be preserved, not by the praise of poets, which may be idle or exaggerated, but

[1] The Spartans have had their day of glorification from rhetoricians and second-hand scholars. To me they have always appeared the most odious impostors in the whole history of antiquity. Even in the military art to which they sacrificed everything else they were repeatedly distanced by others, as witness their discomfiture by the light infantry of the Athenian Iphicrates : and with all their pretentious discipline they produced in the whole course of their wars only two officers who are known to have been gentlemen, Brasidas and Callicratidas. As for their attempts at fine art disclosed by recent excavation, any man with an eye and an elementary historical knowledge of Greek sculpture may judge them.

by the lasting marks of their achievements in history. On this part of the speech we cannot dwell now; but one may be allowed to hope that no Englishman reads it without feeling a glow of something more than cosmopolitan sympathy for the men who delivered Hellas from the invincible armada of the Persian despot, and carried the name and fame of Athens wherever their ships could sail.

"Sons of Athens born in spirit and truth are all born free men ;
    Most of all we, nurtured where the north wind holds his
        reign :
Children all we sea-folk of the Salaminian seamen,
    Sons of them that beat back Persia, they that beat back
        Spain."[1]

The conception of the State, then, was a very living reality to the Athenians among whom Socrates was born and lived. And of the many subjects on which Socrates was never tired of questioning and discoursing, we may suppose that this was not the least interesting to his hearers. Yet we have no direct evidence that he dwelt much on it. We can only suspect from Plato that he had more to say of it than Xenophon lets us know. Xenophon reported only what he could understand, and probably we shall never know what we have lost by Xenophon being a man of timid and commonplace mind—a man who deserved (to say the worst of him at once) to become half a Lacedæmonian and forget how to write Attic. Whatever may be the reason, we find in any case but slender beginnings of political science in the conversations of Socrates as reported by him. The passage where Socrates enforces obedience to the laws as they stand, comparing a citizen who dis-

[1] *Athens*, in Swinburne's *Tristram of Lyonesse*, etc., 1882.

regards the law because it may be changed to a soldier who runs away in battle because there may be peace,[1] may be said to contain a doctrine of civil allegiance. We also find a roughly-sketched classification of forms of government.[2] The names given are royalty (βασιλεία), tyranny, aristocracy, plutocracy, and democracy. The terms monarchy and oligarchy do not occur here, but appear in Plato's *Politicus*. It was Plato likewise who first worked out the theory, lightly touched by Socrates, that government is a special art, and, like all other special arts, can be rightly exercised only by competent persons.[3] This is a branch of the general Socratic doctrine that excellence of every kind, including moral virtue, is analogous to that excellence in particular skilled occupation which, as everybody knows, can be acquired by the appropriate kind of discipline, and cannot be acquired otherwise. Socrates appears to have used this application of the doctrine by way of practical exhortation to those who possessed political power to take politics seriously. Plato developed it into fanciful aspirations, which he himself acknowledged to be impracticable, for government by an absolute and perfectly wise despot, who, not being bound by inflexible general rules, will do what is absolutely fitting in every case that occurs.[4] The elaborate construction of an ideal commonwealth in his *Republic* proceeds on similar principles. Under the actual conditions of life political franchises cannot be

[1] Xen. Mem. iv. 4, 14.
[2] Op. cit. iv. 6, 12.
[3] Op. cit. iii. 9, 10.
[4] Plat. Polit. 294.

adjusted according to political competence, even if an infallible judge of competence could be found : and the only application that can be made of the position laid down by Socrates is to endeavour to secure, as far as may be, that the conditions of competent judgment shall not be wanting to those who must in any case have political power.   Lord Sherbrooke's injunction to educate our masters was thoroughly Socratic both in spirit and in form.

The Platonic *Republic*, I think, must be considered as a brilliant exercise of philosophical imagination, not as a contribution to political science.   Plato's latest work, the *Laws*, appears to have been intended as a kind of compromise between the ideas of the *Republic* and the conditions of practical politics.   In this it was not successful.   Except that it stimulated Aristotle's criticism, it took no definite place in the development of systematic thinking on political matters.   Moreover, it is hardly too much to say that Plato never got to the point of having a theory of the State at all.   In the *Politicus* he seeks to determine the character of the ideal statesman, and touches only by a kind of afterthought on actual and practically possible forms of government. It would be best of all to be governed by a perfectly wise ruler unfettered by any laws whatever ; but it is worst of all to be in the hands of a ruler who has not wisdom and is not restrained by law.   Since the wise governor whom the philosopher desires is hardly to be discovered in the world as it exists, government by fixed laws is accepted as being, though a clumsy business in itself, more tolerable than the tyranny which is the only practical alternative. In the *Republic*, again, Plato starts from the character of individual men and its formation. As a Greek naturally would, and as we have seen that Pericles did, he regarded this as largely depending on the type and institutions of the State in which the individual was a citizen. The individual is for Plato the city in miniature; and to define the notion of justice, the problem by which the dialogue of the *Republic* is opened, and to the solution of which the whole discussion is ostensibly auxiliary, he magnifies the individual into the State. In order to construct the perfect citizen Plato finds himself under the need of constructing the State itself. This point of view left its mark impressed upon the work of Aristotle, in whose treatise on politics, as we now have it, the theory of education occupies one-eighth of the whole : an indefensible arrangement according to modern ideas, giving to the subject, as it does, too much for an incidental consideration, and too little for a monograph. It is better, however, to have one's theory of education not exactly in the right place than to have none at all, which last is about the condition in which we moderns have been, until quite lately, since the tradition of the Renaissance sank into an unintelligent routine.

Aristotle struck out a new and altogether different path. In the first place he made the capital advance of separating ethics from politics. Not only is this not done in the Platonic writings, but the very opposite course is taken in the *Republic :* man is treated as a

micropolis, and the city is the citizen writ large
Another and hardly less important point in Aristotle's
favour is his method of dealing with political facts and
problems. Without abandoning the ideal construction
of the State as it ought to be, he sets himself to make
out the natural history of the State as it is. He begins
not with an ideal, but with the actual conditions of
human society and the formation of governments. He
made a full and minute study of the existing constitutions of Greek cities, and thus collected a great body of
information and materials, unhappily lost to us for the
most part.[1] And we regret the loss the more keenly in
that we know how accurate Aristotle was, and feel more
at home with him than with those who went before him
or came after him. Plato's splendour of imagination
and charm of language have indeed deserted us ; but
we get an exact observation of men and things and a
sound practical judgment, which set us on firm ground
and assure us of solid progress. A balloon is a very
fine thing if you are not anxious to go anywhere in
particular ; a road is common, and the travelling on it
may be tedious, but you come to the journey's end.
Plato is a man in a balloon who hovers over a new land,
and now and then catches a commanding view of its
contours through the mist. Aristotle is the working
colonist who goes there and makes the roads. The
more one considers his work, the more one appreciates
his good sense, his tact in dealing with a question in the
best way possible to him under the given conditions,
and his candour towards the reader. When he does not

[1] The "Constitution of Athens" discovered in our own time is the
one known exception.

see his way to critical analysis, or does not care just then and there to undertake it, and builds upon the data given by common language and opinion, he frankly tells us what he is doing. He always knows exactly what he is undertaking, and works with careful reference to his particular object. His practical insight is very seldom at fault.[1] Even those points in Aristotle's work which are so trite by incessant quotation and allusion that we are now apt to think them obvious have been repeatedly shown to be neither obvious nor superfluous by the most conclusive of all evidence—the mistakes of clever men who have disregarded them.

These merits are conspicuously shown in the general introduction which forms the first book of Aristotle's *Politics*. He plunges without preface, as his manner is, into the analytical inquiry. A State is a community, and every community exists for the sake of some benefit to its members (for all human action is for the sake of obtaining some apparent good): the State is that kind of community which has for its object the most

---

[1] I may mention an instance that occurs to me in detail. In *Eth. Nic.* v. 8 (where, though the book is not of Aristotle's own writing, the matter may be taken as Aristotelian), the harm that may be done by one person to another is classified under four degrees. These are ἀτύχημα, or pure misadventure ; ἁμάρτημα, or injury by negligence, where the harm might have been foreseen (ὅταν μὴ παραλόγως) ; ἀδίκημα, or injury wilful but not premeditated ; and ἀδικία or μοχθηρία, where the injury is deliberate. If the notes taken by me many years ago of the late Mr. Cope's lectures (to which I here acknowledge my great obligation for what I know of the *Politics*) are correct, Mr. Cope thought this last distinction over-refined. But this, as well as the whole classification, corresponds to the gradation attempted by the law of modern civilised countries with a closeness which, considering the rudimentary state of public law in Aristotle's time, deserves admiration rather than criticism.

comprehensive good. The State does not differ from a
household, as some imagine, only in the number of its
members. We shall see this by examining its elements.
To begin at the beginning, man cannot exist in solitude;
the union of the two sexes is necessary for life being
continued at all, and a system of command and obedience for its being led in safety. Thus the relations of
husband and wife, master and servant, determine the
household. Households coming together make a village
or tribe. The rule of the eldest male of the household
is the primitive type of monarchy. Then we get the
State as the community of a higher order in which
the village or tribe is a unity. It is formed to secure
life, it continues in order to improve life.[1] Hence—and
this is Aristotle's first great point—the State is not
an affair of mere convention. It is the natural and
necessary completion of the process in which the family
is a step. The family and the village community are
not independent or self-sufficient; we look to the State
for an assured social existence. The State is a natural
institution in a double sense : first, as imposed on man
by the general and permanent conditions of his life ;
then it is the only form of life in which he can do the
most he is capable of. Man is born to be a citizen—
Ἄνθρωπος φύσει πολιτικὸν ζῷον. There is hardly a
saying in Greek literature so well worn as this; nor
is there any which has worn better, or which better
deserved to become a proverb. It looks simple enough,
but it is one of the truths in which we go on perceiving

[1] γινομένη μὲν τοῦ ζῆν ἕνεκεν, οὖσα δὲ τοῦ εὖ ζῆν.

more significance the more our knowledge increases. This is a thing which happens even in the exact sciences. The full importance of Newton's Third Law of Motion, as enounced and explained by himself, escaped his contemporaries, and was not realised even by the leaders of science until a new light was thrown on it by the development of the modern doctrine of energy. Newton's law, in Newton's own form, was restored by Lord Kelvin and Professor Tait to its rightful place in the forefront of mathematical physics. And we may confidently expect that our children will find more wisdom and light in Charles Darwin's writings than we have as yet found. So, too, in philosophy, "Back to Kant" has become a kind of watchword in Germany. This does not mean that philosophy has been barren ever since Kant, but that the years of a century, even a century remarkable for philosophical interest and activity, were all too short for us to take the full measure of a man of Kant's greatness. And in our present case of Aristotle we may well say that twenty centuries have been none too much; for there have been times once and again when there was sore need of a wise and sober man to cry "Back to Aristotle" to nations deluded by specious political fallacies, and no such man was found.

This axiom of Aristotle contradicts by anticipation the worst and the most widely spread of modern errors, the theory of the Social Contract, which, consistently worked out, can lead to nothing but individualism run mad, until individualism devours itself in giving birth

to a covenanted dictatorship of militarism or capitalism.
Should there be, says Aristotle, a really *cityless* man
(as distinct from one who has lost political standing
by misadventure; Aristotle was probably thinking of
the common case of exile, or of the total subversion
which had befallen his own native city), what can we
say of such an one?   He must be either superhuman
or beneath contempt; he must be in a natural state
of war, with his hand against every man.   Now this
ἄπολις, the clanless and masterless man whom Aristotle
regards as a kind of monster, is identical with the
natural man of Hobbes and Rousseau.   He is the unit
out of whom, if there be only enough of them, theorists
of the Social Contract school undertook to build up
the State.   This is an enterprise at which Aristotle
would have stared and gasped.   We have seen pretty
well what comes of it.   Rousseau and the Social
Contract have had their innings in revolutionary
France; and I think we have by this time ample
warrant of experience for saying that Aristotle was
right, and Hobbes and Rousseau (assuming for the
moment that we have the real mind of Hobbes in
Hobbes as commonly understood) were altogether
wrong.

Thus in Aristotle's view the State is natural and
necessary to man; in the rational order it is even prior
to the individual man, since man cannot live a complete
or tolerable life apart from the State.   Inasmuch as the
State is composed of households, preliminary questions
arise which Aristotle includes in the general term

Economy (the ordering of the οἰκία, which is the com‧ ponent unit of the πόλις); these amount to the study of society apart from the particular form of government. There is nothing, or next to nothing, left to be said about Aristotle's much-discussed defence of slavery, which comes in at this point. The English reader will do well to bear in mind that Aristotle justifies slavery only under conditions which, if applied in practice, would have greatly mitigated the institution as it existed in his time. Of more permanent interest is the sketch of what Aristotle calls the art of trade or wealth-getting (χρηματιστική)—an art which, in his view, is not included in that of the general conduct of social life, but is separate and auxiliary to it. It would be going rather too far to call Aristotle the father of political economy on the strength of this incidental discussion. But it is quite plain that he had a shrewd notion of the scientific handling of economical problems. In particular there are some clear and thoroughly sound remarks on exchange and currency. Lord Sherbrooke (whose bad words for classical studies were after all only *amantium iræ*) cited them with the happiest effect in a paper on Bimetallism. Aristotle goes wrong, indeed, on the matter of the interest of money, and professed moralists and statesmen went wrong for many centuries after him. Our own usury laws were finally repealed as late as 1854. Economy, however, is treated by Aristotle as a purely subordinate study, auxiliary to the general welfare of the State and the promotion of the most desirable type of life.

Modern economists have found it necessary to work out their problems as if wealth were an end in itself, leaving statesmen to take up the results and place them in their due relation to the wider purposes and aims of society. But this leads to some danger of forgetting that there really are other and higher aims in life, and notwithstanding Aristotle's economical errors, we may do well to take a lesson from him herein, or rather from the Greeks : for on this point Aristotle represents the universal feeling of the cultivated Greek society of his time.

Before entering upon any details on his own account, Aristotle clears the way by criticism of some earlier political speculations, Plato's and others. What he says of the community of goods and so forth in Plato's *Republic* is open to the remark that Plato was constructing an ideal which he knew to be impracticable, and Aristotle criticises as if he were dealing with a practical proposal. But the intrinsic value of Aristotle's opinions is not affected by this, nor has it been in any way diminished by the lapse of time and growth of experience. His decisive condemnation of communism remains as forcible, as just, and I fear it must be said as necessary, as ever it was. No one has better expressed what in our own time has been called the magic of ownership. "Carefulness is least in that which is common to most : for men take thought in the chief place for their own, and less for the common stock." Duly regulated private ownership combines the supposed advantages of communism with those of several enjoyment. The higher and only true communism

for men in society is that of the proverb, " Friends
goods are common." How to foster and maintain a
state of generous friendship in which a man shall give
and take in turn of the good things of life, so that
property shall in effect be several in title, but common
in use—that is the high social problem which the
communist evades and the true statesman must attack.
" Moreover, the pleasure we take in anything is increased beyond expression when we esteem it our own;
and I conceive that the individual's affection for himself
is by no means casual, but is of man's very nature." [1]
Aristotle goes on to show that the grievances which are
now the communist's stock in trade, as much as they
were in his time, have no necessary or real connection
with the existence of private property; and in the
course of this criticism he repeats his warning that the
State is not to be considered as a mere magnified
family, nor yet as an alliance of independent and similar
individuals, but as a specific organism made up of divers
parts, all working together, and each fitted for its
own proper function. A scheme for the division of
property among the citizens in equal shares, which had
acquired some reputation in Aristotle's day, is dealt with
by him in the same spirit. He goes straight to the root
of the matter with a piercing question. It is all very
well, he says, to make plans for equal distribution,
or for limiting the amount of property that may be held
by one owner, but supposing it done, the deaths and

[1] Pol. ii. 5, 5-8.

births of a single generation will bring about an altered relation of citizens to property, and upset all your calculations. After the question of property you will have a question of population before you; and how do you mean to dispose of that? Again, it is idle to talk of equality for its own sake, as if it were an absolute good : an equality in pinching poverty would not help us much. Nor would all be done even if you could fix exactly the reasonable and sufficient portion, and give everybody that; "it is of more importance to equalise men's wants than their substance." This is another of Aristotle's deep and pregnant sayings; forgetfulness of it has made shipwreck of many splendid expectations. It would be impracticable in this place, and for the purpose now in hand, to follow into more detail Aristotle's discussion of ideal and actual constitutions. Enough has been said to give some sort of general notion of his critical method.

Still less shall we attempt to follow Aristotle into the special part of his work where he considers the institution of a model State and the several possible types of government. But there remains something of the general part to which we may give a word. The third book of the *Politics* still deals with preliminary questions. It fixes the general terminology and classification of forms of government (which, let us note in passing, have been retained in use ever since), and includes a discussion corresponding to what we now call the theory of sovereignty. One incidental question is, what do we mean by a citizen? Who is a citizen in

the full sense ? The full citizen, in Aristotle's meaning,
is defined by the right to take part in legislation and
the administration of justice. This corresponds with
curious exactness to the old English notion of the
"lawful man"; and it corresponds very nearly to the
modern understanding of political franchises in constitutional countries, though neither Aristotle nor any one
for many centuries later had thought of the indirect
form of legislative power conferred by the right of
sending representatives to form a legislative assembly.
In the Greek view the size of the State was limited by
the number of citizens who could effectually take a direct
part in public affairs. Babylon was all within one wall.
but it was not a city in the proper Greek sense ; that is
not a city which can be taken by an invader at one end
(as the tale went of Babylon) a couple of days before
the other end knows of it.[1] What then constitutes the
identity of a State, since lying within a ring-fence will
not ? Is it continuity of race within the manageable
compass of a State, as the river is the same though the
particles of water are constantly changing ? Neither is
this enough, says Aristotle ; for a tragic and a comic
chorus are not the same, though the men who perform
in them may be the same. Continuity of constitution
is also needful. After a revolution which changes the

[1] Pol. iii. 3, 5. The collection of geographically continuous
parishes covered with buildings in the counties of Middlesex, Surrey,
and Kent, which in 1888 was officially called London, and made an
"administrative county," would have been a hopelessly bewildering
object to an old Greek ; but of one thing he would have been sure,
and rightly, that nothing could well be less like a πόλις.

type of government there is no longer the same State, though it may be called by the same name. Aristotle was obviously not thinking of international relations, which would be entirely confused by applying this test, for example, all treaties to which France was a party would have been annulled over and over again in the course of the nineteenth century. But no theory of the relations of independent States to one another was put into shape until long after this time. From Aristotle's pure natural history point of view there is much to be said for drawing the line where he does.

Again, having defined the citizen and the city, where shall we find our criterion of the merit of particular constitutions? The answer is clear and simple. A normal or right constitution is that which is framed and administered for the common good of all, whether the sovereign power be with one, with few, or with the many. A constitution framed in the exclusive interest of a class, even though it be a majority of the whole, is wrongful and perverse. Royalty, aristocracy, and commonwealth (πολιτεία) are the normal forms; their respective corruptions are tyranny, oligarchy, and democracy—tyranny being a monarchical government worked for the advantage of the monarch over all subjects; oligarchy, the government of a privileged class for the advantage of the rich over the poor; and democracy, the government of the multitude for the advantage of the poor over the rich. *Tyranny* is still always used in a bad sense, and *oligarchy* generally; but as to *democracy* Aristotle's distinction has fallen out of political language, perhaps because his term for the normal state was not specific enough. In English there would be no difficulty in using *commonwealth* or *republic* in Aristotle's good sense, and *democracy* in his bad one; but it has never been done.

A last word may be added on the Greek ideal of the State, if it should still be thought we have nothing to learn from it. Herbert Spencer invited us to look forward to a state of ultimate enlightenment on political matters, in which "law will have no other justification than that gained by it as maintainer of the conditions to complete life in the associated state." This is almost as much as to say that, after all this time, we are at last coming up to the level of Aristotle, or we might indeed say of Pericles. For in Aristotle's view "complete life in the associated state" is precisely the end and aim of government. It is what the city exists for, and a government which does not honestly aim at it has no business to exist. All other ends are subordinate to this. The other ends or reasons assigned in later times would have appeared to Aristotle absurd or irrelevant.[1] In fairness to ourselves, however, we must remember that the problem of modern statecraft is of much greater extent and more formidable complexity than those of Greek political philosophers. After all, the citizens for whose welfare Aristotle conceived the State to exist were, even in the most demo-

---

[1] The *legal* doctrine of the authority of law is a different matter altogether. It belongs to the theory of sovereignty, which we shall come to later.

cratic of constitutions, a limited and privileged class. They are people of leisure and culture, not living by the work of their hands.   To make a true citizen of the worker in mechanical arts, the handicraftsman who has not leisure, is thought by Aristotle a hopeless task, and this even with reference to the skilled and finer kinds of work.   The grosser kind of labour is assumed to be done by slaves, who are wholly outside the sphere of political right.   Not that Aristotle would neglect the welfare of inferior freemen or even of slaves.   He would have the statesman make them comfortable, and bring them as near happiness as their condition admits.   But of happiness in the true sense they are incapable.   We have swept away these restrictions, and find ourselves applying the ideal of a Greek city to our vast and heterogeneous modern political structures—a tremendous extension of the difficulties.   Indeed it may be doubted whether democracy can be called perfect unless there is equality by custom and in fact as well as by law; whether such equality can really be found in any modern commonwealth;[1] and whether it can exist except within a limited and privileged, and therefore homogeneous association.   If we are not much more successful than the Greeks, the task is greater and the aim higher.   It is a lamentable fact that governments still exist which pretend to be civilised, but which, instead of encouraging the completeness of life in their citizens, deliberately hamper or suppress it in many directions, and by the most detestable means.   In

[1] Iceland, I believe, shows the nearest approximation.

such cases, however, it is not that civilisation has failed, but that an essentially barbarous rule has contrived to put on some of its outward appearances. On the other hand, the Greeks can hardly be said to have made any serious progress in the art of governing dependencies; and a continuing union of self-governing colonies with the mother country for purposes of external policy does not seem to have been so much as conceived by them. Aristotle would have found interesting matter in the endeavour towards British imperial organisation which has been carried on for several years with varying but on the whole promising fortune: and, although no sensible Englishman or American affects to treat other civilised nations as inferior, he might have seen some remarkable analogies to the Hellenic sentiment of his own time in the growing ideal of Anglo-Saxon or English-speaking brotherhood.[1]

Aristotle was in a singularly favourable position for his political studies. By circumstances in no way touching his personal credit, he was discharged from taking an active part in public affairs. He could survey the Greek world as a disinterested observer, and the tranquillity produced by the establishment of Macedonian supremacy gave increased opportunities of observation, while the practical extinction of Greek independence had not yet borne its fruit in the visible decay of public life. After Aristotle's time the decay spread rapidly,

[1] These terms are conventional. The bond is in common political institutions and tradition more than in language, and much more than in race. As to the prospects of imperial unity in January 1918 see my article in *Quarterly Review* of that date.

and its effects were striking.   His immediate successors are said to have worked on the theory of politics, but their books are lost, and very little seems to be known of their results.   In the later Greek schools political speculation became stagnant.   The old public spirit was supplanted by a kind of cosmopolitan indifference.   The Roman conqueror was regarded by the Greek rhetoricians as the ruling Englishman in India is now regarded by most Brahmans—as a masterful barbarian sent by the fates, whose acts and institutions were of no importance to the philosophic mind.   There were exceptions among thoughtful Greeks, but I believe it is generally true that no Greek author through the whole period of Roman dominion shows any interest in Latin literature, or treats the Romans as intellectual equals.   Whatever genuine philosophical interest was left ran to the study of ethics, and that as a study regarding the conduct, not of man as a citizen, but simply of man living among men. In many things the post - Aristotelian schools not merely failed to make any advance on what Aristotle had left, but fell back from the point he had reached. Their teaching, as Mr. Newman has said,[1] tended on the whole to detach the individual from politics. Accordingly they contributed to political science nothing worth mentioning.   In Epicurus we may find a rudimentary form of the Social Contract ;[2] and the Stoics had one fine idea, that of the world as a kind of great city in which individual cities were like households

[1] W. L. Newman, The Politics of Aristotle, i. 549.
[2] συνθήκη τις ὑπὲρ τοῦ μὴ βλάπτειν μηδὲ βλάπτεσθαι.

This idea (which is more than once used by Cicero) might, under other conditions, have led them to consider the relations of independent states to one another, and perhaps to develop something like international law. But there were no independent states left; there was only the Roman power which had absorbed all the civilised world, surrounded by dimly known and more or less barbarous tribes and kingdoms. In the early Roman period there is one example of a Greek who made a serious study of Roman institutions, Polybius. His panegyric of the Roman constitution is remarkable as presenting, in a distinct form and concrete application, the theory of mixed and balanced powers which was so much in vogue with British publicists of the eighteenth century, and is hardly yet obsolete among their Continental imitators. In the original Greek form the doctrine is rather concerned with the mixture in one commonwealth of elements belonging to different types.[1]

The Romans were great as rulers and administrators, and they created systematic law. But in philosophy they were simply the pupils and imitators of the Greeks, and showed themselves as little capable of invention in politics as in any other branch. Cicero, a man both of letters and of affairs, devoted a considerable part of

---

[1] A governing assembly maintained by co-optation from special classes of the governed, its executive being appointed from its own number by rotation and having considerable powers, may be an example of a constitution mixed in the Aristotelian, but hardly in the modern sense. The reader may exercise himself in discovering this constitution ; it really exists in certain English societies.

his life to making Latin a philosophical language.   He
succeeded admirably in transcribing the current ideas
of the Greek schools, especially those of the Stoics, in a
language far more attractive and eloquent than that of
his post-Aristotelian models.   More than this he did
not attempt, and in any case did not achieve.   Nobody
that I know of has yet succeeded in discovering a new
idea in the whole of Cicero's philosophical or semi-
philosophical writings ; and the portions of his work on
the Commonwealth which have come down to us in a
fragmentary state are no exception to this.   His theory
was mainly Stoic, and the chief peculiarity of the work
was a pretty full historical discussion of the Roman constitution, which, after the example of Polybius,[1] he
praised as combining the merits of all forms of government.   Even Roman Law, the really great and original
work of Roman intellect, owes something of its theoretical form to Greek philosophy.   It is not our business
to consider in this place whether the debt is of serious
amount.   Jurisprudence is a branch of politics, but too
peculiar a branch for its history to be dwelt on in a
general sketch like the present.   But the Greeks themselves, as we have just said, ceased to produce anything
of vital interest.   The overmastering might of the
Roman empire, levelling men of all kindreds and
nations in a common subjection, finished the work
which the Macedonian supremacy had begun, and with
political independence the scientific study of politics

---

[1] It seems that Cicero had some knowledge of Aristotle's *Politics* ;
Polybius probably had none.   Newman, *op. cit.* ii. xii.-xvi.

became extinct.   It was a sleep of many centuries that
followed, broken only by half-conscious stirrings in the
Middle Ages.   There were brilliant attempts and notable
precursors.   But there was no serious revival of interest
in the theory of politics until the Renaissance; and
the definite new birth of political thinking, and its con-
secutive growth in forms adapted to the civilisation of
modern Europe, may fairly be dated from Hobbes, and
at most cannot be put back earlier than Machiavelli.

II

THE MIDDLE AGES AND THE RENAISSANCE

UNDER the Roman Empire the absence of independent
political life on the one hand, and the vast development
of municipal law and administration on the other, left
no room for theoretical politics. It was enough for the
Roman lawyers that supreme power over the Roman
world had been conferred on Cæsar. So things remained
until the Empire was broken up. On its ruins there
gradually arose a new state of society, and ultimately of
public law. But still the conditions of political philosophy were wanting. The cultivated leisure in which
Greek speculation was nurtured, and which Aristotle
required as the security for even an ordinary citizen's
political competence, had been utterly destroyed, and
awaited reconstruction. The new or renovated institutions that were consolidating the shattered frame of
European civilisation were as yet hardly political in any
proper sense. As Lord Bryce has well said, the Middle
Ages were essentially unpolitical. Only one great
question came into prominence in the thirteenth and

fourteenth centuries, and drew to itself whatever power
or interest men's minds then had in the theoretical
treatment of affairs of State. This was the controversy
between the temporal and the spiritual power. It was
the common ground of the disputants that the Papacy
and the Empire were both divinely ordained, and each in
its own sphere had universal jurisdiction over Christendom. The point of difference was as to the relation
of these two jurisdictions to one another. Was the
temporal ruler in the last resort subordinate to the
spiritual, as the lesser to the greater light? or were their
dignities co-ordinate and equal? The whole reign of
Frederick II., by the confession even of his enemies the
most extraordinary man of his age, was an unremitting
battle between the Roman Emperor and the Roman
Pontiff on this ground. Frederick, who had entered in
his office as the special favourite of the Holy See, found
himself ere long in open hostility to it, and at last
under its formal ban. Indications are not wanting that
he was prepared not only to maintain the independence
of the Empire, but to carry the war into the enemy's
camp. He aimed at nothing less than making himself
supreme in spiritual as well as temporal government.
It seems not clear how far his plans were laid in detail,
but his general intention is certain. He openly treated
the Papal censures as of no authority, and affected in
his own person the titles especially appropriate to
spiritual dominion. He called himself, or encouraged
his followers to call him, the vicar of God on earth, the
reformer of the age, a new Elijah discomfiting the

priests of Baal.   He denounced the Pope as a Pharisee
anointed with the oil of iniquity and sitting in the seat
of corrupt judgment, a false vicar of Christ and deceiv-
ing serpent, who disturbed the world out of mere envy
at the majesty and prosperity of the Empire.   It is
thought that he contemplated the erection of a new
Church in subjection to the Empire, whose centre would
have been in Sicily.[1] The princes and people of Europe
looked by no means unfavourably on Frederick's anti-
papal policy.   But in what seemed its full tide of
success it was cut short by a death almost sudden, and
at the time not free from suspicion.   The excommuni-
cated Emperor's memory was darkened, as was always
the fate of the Roman See's enemies, by the fame of
monstrous heresies and blasphemies.   In his lifetime
these charges got little credence.   St. Louis of France,
the model of Catholic kings, turned a deaf ear to them.
Frederick himself indignantly repudiated and retorted
them.   But he had notoriously committed the un-
pardonable crime of making a treaty on just and equal
terms with the Sultan of Egypt, which indeed was a
sign of political ideas too much in advance of his time
to be acceptable ; and the hostility of a power which
outlives dynasties, and never forgets or forgives,
had its effect in the long run.   Dante felt bound
to place Frederick II. among the unbelievers in
his *Inferno*, though all his sympathies must have

---

[1] Huillard-Bréholles, *Vie et Correspondance de Pierre de la Vigne*,
Paris, 1865.   The learned author draws an ingenious parallel between
Frederick II. and his minister Peter de Vinea and our Henry VIII.
and Thomas Cromwell.

gone with him in his lifelong struggle against the Roman Curia.[1]

The strife which Frederick II. had failed to conclude in action was left as a heritage for the ingenuity of mediæval dialectics. It produced a considerable literature, among which there were two books, one on either side, bearing names of lasting renown. The Papal claims were defended in a treatise *Of the Government of Princes*, begun, but left unfinished, by Thomas Aquinas, and continued by his disciple, Ptolemy of Lucca ; the independence of the Empire was maintained by Dante in his equally celebrated *De Monarchia*.[2] We cannot say that these works develop anything like a complete political theory. So far as they make an approach to this, they show an unconscious reaction from the Aristotelian to the Platonic way of handling the subject. Both the Imperialist and the Papal champion abandon the problem of distributing power on rational principles among the different elements in the State. They fall back on unlimited monarchy as the only means of keeping the peace, and trust to Providence for the ruler being endowed with wisdom.[3] Dante goes even further than St. Thomas. His argu-

[1] The words put into the mouth of Peter de Vinea (*Inf.* xiii. 64-75) afford positive proof, if it were needed.

[2] As to the *De Regimine Principum*, there appears to be no reason to doubt the attribution of the two first books to St. Thomas himself. The third is a later, but not much later, addition ; the fourth is incongruous with the body of the work, and bears the stamp of the Renaissance.

[3] St. Thomas disapproves tyrannicide, but holds that a tyrannical ruler may be justly deposed, at all events in an elective monarchy.

ment is not only for monarchy as the best form of government, but for a universal monarchy, as necessary for the welfare of mankind; and he maintains that the universal monarch, having no rival to fear and no further ambition to satisfy, can have no motive for ruling otherwise than wisely and justly.   The *Monarcha* of Dante's treatise is Plato's heaven-born statesman, the ἀνὴρ βασιλικός, transferred from the Greek city to the larger stage of mediæval Christendom. It is only under his rule, Dante says, that true freedom is possible to men, and this is the justification of his universal dominion.   Aristotle's doctrine, that the merit of a government must be tested by its promotion of the common weal of all the subjects, is fully and expressly adopted.

"Since the Monarch is full of love for men, as was before touched upon, he will have all men good, which cannot be if they live under perverted constitutions:[1] wherefore the Philosopher in his Politics saith, *That in a perverted Commonwealth the good man is a bad citizen; but in a rightful one* good man *and* good citizen *are convertible terms.*   And the aim of such rightful Commonwealths is liberty, to wit that men may live for their own sake.   For citizens are not for the sake of the Consuls, nor a nation for the King; but contrariwise the Consuls are for the sake of the citizens, the King for the sake of the nation.   For as a Commonwealth is not subordinate to laws, but laws to the Commonwealth;

---

[1] "Quod esse non potest apud oblique politizantes," with reference to the παρεκβάσεις of Aristotle's classification.

so men who live according to law are not for the
service of the lawgiver, but he for theirs; which is
the Philosopher's opinion in that which he hath left us
concerning the present matter.   Hence it is plain also
that though a Consul or King in regard of means be the
lords of others, yet in regard of the end they are the
servants of others : and most of all the Monarch, who
without doubt is to be deemed the servant of all."

We are not concerned here with the scholastic arguments in favour of monarchy, drawn from the intrinsic
excellence of unity as compared with plurality, which
are used both by Dante and by St. Thomas ; nor can
we dwell at length on Dante's reasons for identifying
his ideal monarch with the actual prince who wore the
crown of the revived Western Empire.   They deserve
some passing mention, however, if only to show what
had taken the place of political science in even the best
minds of the time: There is nothing more curious in
literature than the proof in the second book of the
De Monarchia that the Roman people were ordained of
God to conquer the world.   The Psalmist, Aristotle,
Cicero, Virgil, and Aquinas are cited as equally relevant
and binding authorities; and the application of the
language of the second Psalm to the Roman dominion
is almost as strong as anything addressed to Frederick
II. by his Chancellor and courtiers.   It is argued that
the Roman victories over all the other powers of the
earth were not mere vulgar conquests, but due and
formal trials by battle of the dispute for universal
sovereignty, the result of which declared the judgment

of God.[1]   Most curious of all is the argument that the
title of the Roman Empire was confirmed by the highest
possible authority in the passion of Christ.   The sin of
Adam was punished in Christ, but there is no punishment without competent jurisdiction; and, since Christ
represented all mankind, a jurisdiction extending to all
mankind was in this case the only competent one.
Such a universal jurisdiction was that of Rome as
exercised by Pilate.   In the third and last book Dante
proves that the authority of the Roman Empire proceeds
immediately from God, and is not held of the Pope or
the Church.   His minute refutations of the reasons
adduced on the Papal side from the sun and moon, the
offerings of the Magi, the two swords, and so forth, now
seem to us only one degree less grotesque than the
reasons themselves.

Yet there is an earnest endeavour in this work of
Dante's, though it is but feeling about in a dim twilight,
to find a solid ground for a real system of European
public law.   The monarch he conceives is not a
universal despot, but a governor of a higher order set
over the princes and rulers of particular states, and
keeping the peace between them.   He is to have the
jurisdiction, in modern language, of an international
tribunal.   "Wheresoever contention may be, there judgment ought to be;" and therefore the monarch is need-

---

[1] The "formalia duelli" prescribed by Dante as the conditions of a
just and judicially decisive war are, as might be expected, extremely
vague.   As to the early history of trial by battle see Fustel de Coulanges,
La Monarchie Franque, p. 453, and Mr. George Neilson's *Trial by
Combat*, and cp. Pollock and Maitland, *Hist. Eng. Law*, ii. 597, 630
(600, 632 in 2nd edition).

ful to give judgment in the contentions which arise
between independent princes.   The desire for such an
authority had not apparently been felt by the Greek
philosophers.   Dante says nothing of the manner in
which the Emperor's jurisdiction is to be exercised, or
of the means whereby his judgments are to be executed.
He must have known that his idea was far removed
from anything likely to be put in practice.   Even
now we have made only the first steps towards realis-
ing it.   Still the idea was a noble one, and we may
say for it of Dante, in his own words concerning his
master Virgil—

> "Onorate l'altissimo poeta."

For the rest, we must say of all the mediæval writers
on politics, as we said before of Plato, but in a much
more unqualified sense, that they really have no theory
of the State.   Their aim is to maintain the cause of the
Papacy or of the Empire as the case may be.   Disinterested study of politics was a thing beyond them.
Our own Bracton (or some one who amplified his text not
long after it was written) has elements of a constitutional doctrine, but such beggarly elements as only to
show the poverty of the age in systematic thought on
such matters.   He rejects the notion of an English king
being an absolute sovereign.   The king is under the
law, and if he attempts to govern against law, the great
men of the land who are his companions must do some·
thing to check him.   But how the check is to be
applied we are not told : much less where, if not

in the Crown, the ultimate political authority really
is. Marsiglio of Padua, who wrote early in the
fourteenth century,[1] shows a certain return to Aristotelian method and results, as well as familiarity with
the *Politics*, of which he adopts the terminology.
He defended government by the majority by the same
argument that Aristotle had already used as applicable
to the imperfect condition of actually existing com-
munities. True it is that the people at large are not fit
to govern; but they can tell whether they are well or
ill governed, as a man knows whether his shoe fits him
or not without being a shoemaker. In one passage there
is a suggestion of representative government, or at any
rate the framing of laws by elected representatives.
Marsiglio likewise distinctly marked the separation of
the executive power (which he calls by its modern
name) from the legislative; moreover, he advocated a
complete separation of temporal from spiritual authority,
and would have the temporal laws and magistrates
make no difference of persons on the score of religious
opinion. Being a zealous Imperialist, Marsiglio proceeded to deny the pre-eminence of the Roman See

---

[1] His book was first printed, it seems at Basel, in the sixteenth century (opus insigne cui titulum fecit autor Defensorem Pacis, etc. *s.l.*
1522). In the British Museum Catalogue it has to be sought under the
title *Menandrinus*, a Latinised form of his surname, which, however,
the Bodleian catalogue censures as erroneous. Our countryman
William of Ockham's gigantic Dialogue, practically accessible only in
Goldast's eighteenth-century collection *Monarchia*, came next in
importance to Marsiglio. He was sure the people of Rome had a
natural right, and thought they had a divine right, to elect their own
bishop. It seems that Wycliffe used his work.

even in spiritual matters, and naturally incurred ex-communication. Half a century later his steps were followed with no small vigour and effect (but this time for Gallican and patriotic rather than Imperial ends) in the French dialogue known as the *Songe du Verger*, or in Latin *Somnium Viridarii*,[1] of which the authorship is now attributed to Philippe de Mézières.[2]

The modern study of politics, however, begins with Machiavelli. Not that he made any definite or permanent contribution to political theory which can be laid hold of as a principle fertile of new consequences. His works are more concerned with the details of state-craft than with the analysis of the State. But we find in him, for the first time since Aristotle, the pure passion-less curiosity of the man of science. We find the separation of Ethics and Politics, which had fallen into neglect, not only restored, but forming the groundwork of all Machiavelli's reasoning, and made prominent even to the point of apparent paradox and scandal. Machia-velli takes no account of morality. He assumes cer-

[1] It is a distorted version of a Latin dialogue by Giov. da Legnano. See G. d. L. *Tractatus de bello*, etc., ed. Holland, 1917 (Carnegie Institution). The French text ("Le songe du vergier qui parle de la disputacion du clerc et du chevalier") was first printed at Lyons by Jacques Maillet in 1491. The only modern edition is in vol. ii. of *Traitez des droits et libertez de l'Eglise Gallicane*, 1731. The Latin version was published in Paris in 1516. The dialogue form and the interlocutors appear to have been borrowed from William of Ockham's *Disputatio inter clericum et militem super potestate praelatis ecclesiae atque principibus terrarum commissa*.

[2] Gierke, *Staats. u. Korporationslehre des Alterthums u. d. Mittelalters*, p. 507; *Revue Historique*, May 1892. But see Ducoudray, *Les origines du Parlement de Paris*, 1902, p. 137.

tain ends to be in the view of a prince or nation.
They might be, we know by his own life and sufferings
that often they were, ends of which Machiavelli himself
disapproved.   But he considers, as a purely intellectual
problem, by what means an Italian ruler of the sixteenth century is most likely to attain those ends.
Religion and morality are in his assumed point of view
simply instruments in the hand of the ruler ; not
masters, not always even safe guides, but useful servants and agents.   The art of politics depends on the
constant principles and motives of human self-interest.
Its details are to be learnt from history and experience.
Machiavelli's own account of his best known (though
perhaps not his most important) work, as he gave it in
a familiar letter to his friend Francesco Vettori, leaves
nothing to desire in clearness as far as it goes.   The
letter describes how he spends the day in out-of-door
pursuits ; fowling in the season, or looking after his
wood-cutting, and then gossiping or playing cards at the
roadside inn nearest his country retreat, picking up news
and noting men's various humours.   But his time of
real pleasure is in the evening; then he casts off his
rough and muddy country dress, and arrays himself as
becomes a statesman in good company; his company
are the ancients, among whose history and thoughts he
spends this time, forgetting misfortune and poverty.
He has meditated over what he learns from these companions, and set down the chief results.   " I have made,"
he says, " a treatise, *De Principatibus*, where I go to the
depth of my ability into the consideration of this matter,

discussing what is the nature of sovereignty,[1] what
kinds of it there are, how they are acquired, how maintained, and for what causes lost." He describes his
treatise, that is, as a study of pure natural history, an
inquiry by what means despotic rulers (such as then
abounded in Italy, some of greater, some of smaller pre-
tensions) are, in fact, successful or unsuccessful in consolidating their power.   And that is exactly what the
book is on the face of it.   Machiavelli does not approve
or advise fraud and treachery, as he has been charged
with doing.   His own public conduct, so far as known
(and he was a public servant for many years), was up-
right both abroad and at home.   He only points out
that power gained in certain ways must be maintained,
if at all, by corresponding means.   It is not strange that
a man living among Italian politics, such as they then
were, and as they were closely observed and described
by himself, should regard the separation of policy from
morality as a remediless evil which must be accepted.
There is no ground for saying that he did not perceive it to
be an evil at all.   Nor is it to be set down as the evil fruit
of his advice that other despots and usurpers in later times
have been successful by those arts which Machiavelli
described as leading to success.   No man ever learnt
the secret of despotism out of a book.

It has always been assumed, however, that Machia-

[1] Machiavelli's *Principato* is not easy to translate exactly.   He
means by it every form of personal government, under whatever title,
as opposed to popular government (*repubblica*) : these being the only
two kinds into which he thinks it worth while for his purposes to
divide governments in general.

velli had some further object in his political writings: and much controversial ingenuity has been expended on determining what it was. All kinds of opinion have been advanced, from the vulgar prejudice that Machiavelli was a cynical counsellor of iniquity to the panegyric of the modern writers who place Machiavelli with Dante and Mazzini as one of the great preparers and champions of Italian unity.[1] This latter view contains at all events more truth than the old one. Machiavelli, though by education and preference a Republican, despaired of a strong and stable republican government in the Italian States as he knew them. The one pressing need for the restoration of prosperity to Italy was to deliver her from the invaders, French, German, and Spanish, who spoiled and ruined her: and this could be done, as it seemed to Machiavelli, only by some Italian prince wiser, more fortunate, and more nobly ambitious than others making himself the chief power in Italy, and gathering such strength of native arms as would enable him to withstand the foreigner. For an end so sacred in Italian eyes all the political means of the time were justified; and beside the possibility of attaining it questions of municipal politics and forms of domestic government sank into insignificance. National unity and independence was to be made the supreme aim, even if it had to be attained through a military despotism. We, who have seen German unity

---

[1] F. Costèro, Preface to *Il Principe*. Milan, etc., 1875. See further J. A. Symonds, *Ency. Brit.* 9th ed. *s.v.* Machiavelli, and Lord Acton's and Mr. Burd's introductions to Mr. Burd's edition of *Il Principe*, Oxford, 1891, and cp. T. Whittaker, *The Theory of Abstract Ethics*, 1916, p. 100.

accomplished (allowing for differences of civilisation and manners) in almost exactly the same fashion that Machiavelli conceived for Italy, can at any rate not suppose that his idea was chimerical. That such was indeed one of his leading ideas is beyond doubt. It is not only avowed in the last chapter of the *Prince*, but the subordination of internal to external politics throughout Machiavelli's work is explicable by this fixed purpose, and by this only. For Machiavelli as for Dante, the question of assuring political life at all is still pressing to be solved before there is time to consider narrowly what is the best form of it. In Aristotle's phrase, the process of γίγνεσθαι τοῦ ζῆν ἕνεκεν is as yet barely accomplished, and the final problem of εὖ ζῆν is thrust into the background. Therefore even Machiavelli, full as he is of observation and practical wisdom, is only on the threshold of political science. His doctrine is a theory of the preservation of States rather than a theory of the State.[1]

In Jean Bodin's treatise *Of Commonwealth* we get for the first time the definite enunciation of at least one capital point of modern political doctrine. He is entitled, indeed, to share with Hobbes the renown of having founded the modern theory of the State; and it may be said of him that he seized on the vital point of it at the earliest time when it was possible. The doctrine referred to is that of political sovereignty. In every independent community governed by law there

[1] Or in more technical terms: "Machiavelli's field is *Politik*, not *Staatslehre*": Dunning, *History of Political Theories*, 1902, p. 293.

must be some authority, whether residing in one person
or several, whereby the laws themselves are established,
and from which they proceed.   And this power, being
the source of law, must itself be above the law : not
above duty and moral responsibility, as Bodin carefully
explains; but above the municipal ordinances of the particular State—the positive laws, in modern phrase—
which it creates and enforces. Find the person or persons
whom the constitution of the State permanently invests
with such authority, under whatever name, and you have
found the sovereign.   "Sovereignty is a power supreme
over citizens and subjects, itself not bound by the laws."
This power somewhere is necessary to an independent
State, and its presence is the test of national independence.   Such is in outline the principle of sovereignty as
stated by Bodin, taken up and enlarged a century later
by Hobbes, and adopted by all modern publicists with
only more or less variation in the manner of statement.
It is one of the things which appear tolerably simple to
a modern reader.   The history of English politics and
legislation has made it specially acceptable to English
readers, and to an English lawyer it needs a certain effort
of imagination to conceive that people ever thought
otherwise.   Yet a little consideration will make it
equally obvious that the proposition could not have
assumed a definite shape much before the sixteenth
century.   The legal supremacy of the State is conceivable only when the State has acquired a local habi-
tation and a permanent establishment.   The mediæval
system of Europe was not a system of States in our

sense or in the Greek sense. It was a collection of
groups, held together in the first instance by ties
of personal dependence and allegiance, and connected
among themselves by personal relations of the same
kind on a magnified scale. Lordship and homage,
from the Emperor down to the humblest feudal tenant,
were the links in the chain of steel which saved the
world from being dissolved into a chaos of jarring
fragments. The laws and customs which were obeyed
by princes and people, by lords and their men, were
not thought of as depending on the local government
for their efficacy. The Roman law, in particular,
was treated as having some kind of intrinsic and
absolute authority. We see its influence even in
England, where it was never officially received. Men
sought in the shadow of the Roman Empire and its dead
institutions the unity of direction and government
which their actual life had not yet found. The old unity
of the clan had disappeared, and it was only gradually
and slowly, as kingdoms were consolidated by strong
rulers, that the newer unity of the nation took its place.
Here and there, as in England, where a clear territorial
definition was from an early time assured by the
geographical nature of things, and foreign disturbance
was easily kept aloof, a true national feeling and life
rose up soon and waxed apace. But on the Continent
the fifteenth century was still a time when nations were
forming rather than formed ; and when in the suc-
ceeding century the French monarchy began to feel its
real strength, the masterly definitions of Bodin gave

expression to a change in the political face of Europe
which was yet young.

Here the question occurs whether, as Hobbes and his
followers have maintained or assumed, sovereign power
in this sense must be unlimited, single and indivisible.
Can there be divers authorities within one State, each
of them supreme in its own sphere? As matter of
fact, the answer is that it not only may be but must
be so under any federal constitution, as every instructed
Australian or Canadian citizen well knows, and
American publicists have known much longer. A
statute of Rhode Island made in due form and within the
powers reserved to State legislatures by the Constitution cannot be legally overruled by any human
authority, while an Act of Congress duly made in
exercise of the powers conferred on the federal legislature must be obeyed in Rhode Island whether the men
of Rhode Island like it or not. It is true that the
Constitution itself provides ways of amendment,
purposely made elaborate and difficult : and some men
would say that the amending authority is the real
sovereign. That authority not only is very seldom
active, but has no power to legislate in detail for any
State. It can add articles to the federal Constitution ;
it cannot enact a new statute for Rhode Island. Such
an indirect and remote control is not the sovereignty
of practical politics. If we must find a single authority
"not bound by the laws" in any sense whatever, we
must go back to an undefined and unorganised body,
the people of the United States from whom the Con-

stitution itself proceeded. If we deny that there is
any real sovereign power in the United States or in
the Commonwealth of Australia, we reduce sovereignty
to a mere logical figment having no useful relation to
facts. These points cannot be fully worked out here;
but it is well to give a taste of them before we come to
deal with Hobbes.[1]

Bodin was a man of vast learning, and, with one
strange exception,—his polemic against sorcerers,—it
was an enlightened learning. On public economy and
many other matters his opinions were far in advance of
those current in his age. He not only strove to put in
practice, but distinctly announced as a necessary
principle, the foundation of political theory on a broad
base of historical observation. Like Machiavelli, he
showed in his own conduct as a citizen a settled attach-
ment to freedom and justice, and suffered for his con-
stancy. Yet we find in Bodin's doctrine, as in that of
Machiavelli before him and Hobbes after him, a certain
apparent leaning in favour of absolute power. He not
only defines sovereignty as a power not subject to the
laws, but, on the contrary, maker and master of them—
a power which so far may belong[2] to one, to few, or to
many, to a king, to an assembly, or to both together—
but he is prone to identify the theoretical sovereign with
the actual king in States where a king exists. For his

---

[1] See "The Nature of Sovereignty" in Bryce, *Studies in History
and Jurisprudence*, 1901, ii. 49-111.

[2] Bodin regarded sovereignty, with a surviving touch of mediæval
realism, as a kind of estate or dignity capable of being possessed and
granted in the full technical sense of those terms.

own country this might be done without grave difficulty:
but Bodin was not content without foreign instances,
and England, even when in the hands of the Tudors the
power of the Crown had reached its utmost height, gave
him a great deal of trouble. He recognises more fairly
than Hobbes the possibility of a limited monarch. The
Emperor, he says, is no absolute sovereign, for he is
bound by the ordinances and decrees of the German
princes. Probably Bodin's position is to be accounted
for by his practical view of the French monarchy.
Doubtless the king's power appeared to him, as indeed
it was, the only one then capable of governing France
with tolerable efficiency and equity. And it is curious
to see what limits Bodin, herein less rigidly consistent
than Hobbes, proceeds to impose on monarchical power
after he has defined it as unlimited. Sovereign authority,
as we have seen, is the absolute power in the State
wherever that may be. It is that power which is neither
temporary, nor delegated, nor subject to particular rules
which it cannot alter,[1] nor answerable to any other power
on earth. " Maiestas nec maiore potestate, nec legibus
ullis, nec tempore definitur . . . princeps populusque in
quibus maiestas inest rationem rerum gestarum nemini

[1] Yet if it has rules of procedure, as every composite or numerous
body must have, its acts will not be recognized unless they are regular ;
and in making new rules it must proceed according to the existing
ones. The question is not whether any one can punish a sovereign
body for irregularity, but whether irregular action will be treated as
binding. "Suppose King, Lords, and Commons should meet in one
chamber and vote together, an order passed by them would not be
obeyed by the English people": John C. Gray, *The Nature and
Sources of the Law*, 1909, s. 173.

præterquam immortali Deo reddere coguntur." [1]   And such power, as matter of legal and historical fact, belongs to the kings of France.   But this only means that they have no legal duties to their subjects.   They have moral duties, or, as Bodin says in the language of the juris-prudence of his day, they remain bound by the law of nature : " Quod summum in Republica imperium legibus solutum diximus, nihil ad divinas aut naturæ leges pertinet."   Thus an absolute prince is bound in moral duty and honour by his conventions with other princes and rulers, and even with his own subjects.   In certain cases he is bound by the promises of his predecessors ; though no sovereign power (as ancient writers had already seen) can bind its successors in the sense of making a law that shall be unalterable and of perpetual obligation.   Bodin shows at some length, and with much perspicuity, both on principle and by historical examples, the idleness of assuming to make laws irrevoc-able.   The sovereign power could, it is admitted, repeal the law but for the clause forbidding repeal.   But such a clause is itself part of the law, so that the sovereign can repeal the body and the supposed safeguard of the law together.   If there is a legislative power which cannot do this, it is not really sovereign.   Thus Bodin distinguished legal obligation in the strict sense from purely moral and honourable duties on the one hand, and from the duties created by convention between independent powers on the other, and thereby made

---

[1] Bodin's own Latin version of his work is really a new recension and is fuller and more precise in language than the French.

a great step towards the clear separation of the legal from the ethical sphere of thought within political science itself—a thing only less in importance than Aristotle's original separation of Politics from Ethics.

But Bodin shrinks from the extreme consequences to which Hobbes pursued a similar conception. He tells us of organic laws or rules which may be so closely associated with the very nature of this or that sovereignty that they cannot be abrogated by the sovereign power itself, and he instances the rule of succession to the French crown. Again, there are institutions of society, such as the family and property, which he assumes as the foundation of the State; and with these even the sovereign power cannot meddle.[1] From the inviolability of property he draws the consequence that not the most absolute monarch can lawfully tax his subjects without their consent. At this day we should say that these are excellent maxims of policy, but do not affect the State's legal supremacy, or (to anticipate the classical English name for the thing as it appears in our own constitution) the omnipotence of Parliament. There are things which no ruler in his senses would do, things which very few or none can afford to do. Just so there are many things a private man is legally entitled to do which he will not do if he is wise, or which no man of common sense or common good feeling will do. But his legal right is

---

[1] Bodin charges Aristotle with omitting the family from his definition of the State. As Aristotle explicitly leads up to the State from the family, and defines the family as the unit of the State, it is difficult to see what Bodin meant.

not thereby affected. And so, too, particular authorities in the State may have legal powers which are in practice never exercised, and which it would be impolitic to exercise in almost any conceivable case. There is no doubt that in England the King is legally entitled to refuse assent to a Bill passed by both Houses of Parliament, though such a thing has not been done for about two centuries, and as far as human foresight can go will never be done again. As a harsh or foolish exercise of legal or political rights does not cease to be within the agent's right because it is harsh or foolish, so an unwise or morally wrongful act of sovereign power is not the less an act of sovereign power because it is unwise or wrong. Bodin's doctrine, expressed in modern terms, would be that constitutional limitations as to the form of government may be imposed by custom as well as by a written instrument; whereas Hobbes said he could never understand what a fundamental law signified. Something very like a doctrine of undefined constitutional limitations was current in England till the eighteenth century, but never had practical effect.

Bodin's opinions in matters of detail are for the most part worthy of his exposition of leading principles. He condemned slavery without reserve, and advocated a comprehensive toleration of religious opinion. Not only did he anticipate, as we have just seen, the analytical method of Hobbes; he anticipated the historical method of Montesquieu by a detailed discussion of the influence of climate and geographical conditions on political

institutions and government.   His work attained a great
reputation in a short time.   Besides the author's own
Latin version, an English translation appeared early in the
seventeenth century.   There is little doubt that Bodin
not only prepared the way for Hobbes and Montesquieu,
but that both of them—writers differing from one another
as widely as possible in method, manner, and purpose
—actually studied and profited by him.

Turning to England, we find attempts in speculative
politics arising out of the study of the English constitution and laws as early as the fifteenth century.   Fortescue, both in his book *De laudibus legum Angliæ* and
in his less known treatises on the Law of Nature and
the Monarchy of England,[1] is careful to represent the
king's power as not absolute but limited by the law, or,
to use the language borrowed by him from St. Thomas
Aquinas's *De Regimine Principum*, not "royal" but "political."   The king is the head of the body politic, but
can act only according to its constitution and by the
appropriate organs in each case.   And it is said in
general terms that the king's power is derived from
the consent of the people.   But the question where
political supremacy really lies is not followed up.

---

[1] Fortescue's *Monarchia*, otherwise "On the Governance of England,"
was critically edited for the Oxford University Press in 1885 by Mr.
C. Plummer, with an introduction and notes abounding in excellent
learning on mediæval history and politics.   For the relation of
Fortescue's doctrine to Lancastrian policy see Stubbs, *Const. Hist.*
iii. §§ 364, 365.   His conception of a true limited monarchy as
"dominium politicum et regale" seems to have been original ; the
common opinion was that only elective kings could have limited
authority.

Neither is any definite theory of the origin of government put forward.   More's *Utopia* calls for mention on account of its literary fame ; but, though it contains incidentally not a few shrewd criticisms, open and covert, on the state of English society in the first quarter of the sixteenth century, we cannot count it as an addition to political science.   It is a Platonic or ultra-Platonic fancy, bred of the Platonism of the Renaissance.   Even more than the *Republic* of Plato it belongs to the poetry as distinguished from the philosophy of politics.   In the *De Republica Anglorum* or *English Commonwealth* of Sir Thomas Smith, first published after the author's death in 1583,[1] we find something much more like a forerunner of Hobbes. Indeed, so clear and precise are Smith's chapters on Sovereignty that one is tempted to think he must somehow have had knowledge of Bodin's work.   At the outset he defines political supremacy in a manner by no means unlike Bodin's.   "To rule is understood to have the highest and supreme authority of commandment.   That part or member of the commonwealth is said to rule which doth control, correct and direct all other members of the commonwealth."   When he comes to English institutions in particular, he states the omnipotence of Parliament in the most formal manner, and so far as I know for the first time, as if on purpose to contradict Bodin's argument that the monarchy of England is really

---

[1] Ed. L. Alston, Cambridge, 1906.   Mr. Alston endeavours, I think with mistaken ingenuity, to minimize the importance of the classical passage on Parliament here quoted.   It was Tudor policy to exalt the power of Parliament, and Smith had been a Secretary of State.

absolute. "The Parliament abrogateth old laws, maketh new, giveth order for things past and for things hereafter to be followed, changeth right and possessions of private men, legitimateth bastards, establisheth forms of religion, altereth weights and measures, giveth form of succession to the crown, defineth of doubtful rights whereof is no law already made. . . . And to be short, all that ever the people of Rome might do, either *Centuriatis Comitiis* or *tributis*, the same may be done by the Parliament of England; which representeth and hath the power of the whole realm, both the head and body." It is true that Bodin's *De Republica* was published only in 1577, the year of Smith's death. But we know that Smith's work was composed while he was ambassador at the French Court, and considering how long books often waited for publication at that time, we may fairly suppose that Bodin's treatise, or at least the introductory part of it, was already in existence, and that a certain number of scholars were acquainted with its contents. Even a century later a great deal of private communication of this kind went on.[1] Sir Thomas Smith's principles, wherever he got them, have the merit of being much the clearest which down to that time had been put into shape by an English author or in the English language.

We now come to Hobbes, with whom the modern school of political theory begins. Aristotle effected the separation of Ethics from Politics. From Hobbes, or

[1] It is hardly probable that there was any personal meeting, nor is there any need to suppose one.

rather through Hobbes, we get the further separation of
policy from legality—of that which is wise or expedi-
ent from that which is allowed by positive law. The
political theory of Hobbes runs more or less through
everything that he wrote, but is especially contained in
his *Leviathan*.[1]   This famous and much decried treatise
contains a great deal of curious learning of all sorts,
including not a few theological eccentricities. But the
principles laid down by Hobbes which have had a
serious effect upon later political thinking may be reduced to two.   One of these is the principle of
sovereignty; the other is the theory of the origin of
civil society in contract. We have already seen the
doctrine of sovereignty as it was stated in the preceding
century by Bodin.   With him it rested on a pure
analysis of the fact of civilised government. In every
form of government you must come at last to some
power which is absolute, to which all other powers of
the State are subject, and which itself is subject to none.
The possession of such power is sovereignty, and the
person or body in whom it resides is sovereign.
Hobbes is in one respect less enterprising and straight-
forward than Bodin.   In his anxiety to fortify the
doctrine of sovereignty and to leave no excuse for
disputing the authority of the State, he gives an
elaborate account of the construction of the State by
an original covenant between its members. Some

[1] Some further details may be found in papers of mine on Hobbes,
National Review, September 1894, and Hobbes and Locke, *Journ. Soc.
Comp. Legisl.*, 1908. The earlier book, *De Cive* (in Hobbes's own English
version, *Elements of Government and Civil Society*), is rather less dogmatic.

such imaginary covenant, modified in its terms and circumstances according to the conclusion which the particular author sought to establish, was already current in the Reformation controversies and was familiar to later publicists as the Original or Social Contract: as we have already noticed,[1] the conception of it goes much farther back. In Hobbes's form there is no agreement between the ruler and the subject, only an agreement among the subjects to place or leave all power in his hands, and this is vital to the scheme of the *Leviathan*. If we are called upon to say in one sentence what Hobbes did, we must say that he supported a plain and sound doctrine by needless and untenable fiction, and for the purpose of deducing consequences from it which it would not bear. This, however, is no more than has to be said of many of the most able men in all ages. Hobbes's firm grasp of all his ideas, and the admirable clearness with which his arguments and results, whether right or wrong, are invariably stated, make him the first classic of English political science.

Let us now see how Hobbes goes to work to construct the State. Men, taking them all round, are by nature equal, none being so strong in body or mind that he need not be in fear of others, or so weak that he may not be dangerous to them. Men living without any common power set over them would be in a state of mutual fear and enmity, that is, in a state of war. Such a state of things in permanence would be intoler-

[1] P. 30 above.

able; in it there is no property, no law, and no justice. Every man will aim at securing his own safety, and for that purpose will take all he can get. Peace is good, but life is necessary, and in the state of war it is our right to use all means to defend ourselves.

The only way to peace is for men to abandon so much of their natural rights as is inconsistent with living in peace. This again can be done only by mutual agreement; and the faithful performance of such an agreement, as evidently tending to self-preservation, is a rule of reason, or in the terms of the Schoolmen which Hobbes adopts in his own sense, a law of nature. But a mere agreement to live together in peace is insufficient. Men's individual passions and ambitions would speedily break up a society resting on no better foundation. There must be " a common power to keep them in awe, and to direct their actions to the common benefit." This is effected by all the members of the community giving up their natural rights to some man or body of men in whom their united power is henceforth to be vested. Every member of the community gives up to the chosen head the right of governing himself on condition that every other member does the same. The person or body so invested with the power of the whole becomes a kind of new person; "and he that carrieth this person is called *sovereign*, and hath sovereign power; and every one besides, his *subject*."

It is by no means easy to make out whether Hobbes intended this to be taken as a true account of the

manner in which civil governments had been established as a matter of fact.   I think he would have been
prepared to say that it would make no difference to his
argument whether it were so or not; at any rate, he is
prepared to show to any one who presumes to traverse
the story of the original covenant that if he disputes it
he has no title to live in society at all.   Hobbes proceeds to deduce from this institution of the Commonwealth, as he calls it, the attributes of sovereignty.
The sovereign's authority is derived from the consent
of the subjects, and he is their agent for the purpose of
directing their united strength for the common benefit;
but he is an agent with unlimited discretion, and with
an authority which cannot be revoked.   The subjects
cannot change the form of government, for that would
be a breach of the original covenant both in respect
of the sovereign and towards one another.   The
sovereign cannot forfeit his power, for he made no
covenant, and there is none therefore which he can
break.[1]   It is true that no promise is made to him,
but there is no need of it; his authority is enforce-
able not by any covenanted right but by the natural
right or power which the subjects' mutual covenant
has left to him and him alone.   Any subject who
dissents from the institution of the sovereign thereby
ceases to be a member of the community and remits
himself to the original state of war, in which any

---

[1] Some earlier writers had maintained that the natural obligation
of keeping faith was strong enough to support a subsequent promise
by the ruler to his subjects.   But this would not suit Hobbes.

one who can may destroy him without violating any right. For similar reasons the sovereign is irresponsible and unpunishable. No man can complain of what his agent does within the authority given him, and in the case of a political sovereign all acts of sovereignty have been authorised beforehand by all the subjects. Holders of sovereign power may commit iniquity but not injustice. The sovereign, again, is the sole judge of what is necessary for the defence and security of the commonwealth, and, in particular, of the question what doctrines are fit to be taught in it. There are likewise annexed to sovereignty the powers of legislature and judicature, of making war and peace, of choosing counsellors and officers, of rewarding and punishing, and of regulating titles and precedence. All these rights are indivisible and incommunicable; the sovereign may delegate them, but cannot abandon them.[1] Hobbes is perfectly aware that the sovereign thus defined need not be one man; but he is nevertheless anxious to show that in England the king alone is sovereign. Yet in his principal work he gives very little express argument to this topic, which is worked out separately in the dialogue entitled *Behemoth*. He purports to show, as Bodin had done before him, that sovereign power cannot be divided, and this he seems to think fatal to all doctrines of mixed or limited monarchy. The loose language of some constitutional

---

[1] This was the point of agreement between Hobbes and the partisans of divine right. Filmer spoke of his work with much respect.

advocates is taken by him as stamping their cause itself with repugnance to the nature of things. It does not occur to him as possible that sovereignty should be vested in a compound as well as in a simple body; still less does he conceive that legal power, the formal authority of enacting indisputable commands, should reside in one part of the Commonwealth, and the political supremacy which in fact wields the legal power in another; as, in England, the legislative power of Parliament is guided by the Cabinet and ultimately controlled by the majority of the House of Commons.

The limits of sovereignty, or the liberty of the subject, as they may be indifferently called in Hobbes's view, are defined as consisting in those powers or rights of the individual man which he cannot surrender by any covenant. Thus no man can be bound to kill himself, to abstain from self-preservation, or to accuse himself; and more generally the obligation of subjects to the sovereign lasts no longer than he has power to protect them.

Hobbes's further consideration of civil laws gives him occasion to enter more in detail upon the relation of the sovereign power in a State to its municipal laws. His definition, with its introductory explanation, really contains all the points which were developed in the course of the nineteenth century by the English school of jurisprudence.

" Law in general is not counsel but command; nor a command of any man to any man; but only of him

whose command is addressed to one formerly " (*i.e.*
already, by having agreed to be his subject) " obliged to
obey him.   And as for civil law, it addeth only the
name of the person commanding, which is *persona
civitatis*, the person of the Commonwealth.

   " Which considered, I define civil law in this manner.
Civil law is to every subject those rules which the
Commonwealth hath commanded him by word, writing,
or other sufficient sign of the will, to make use of for
the distinction of right and wrong; that is to say, of
what is contrary and what is not contrary to the
rule."

   Right and wrong, in the legal sense, are that which
the law of the State allows[1] and forbids, and nothing else.
To understand this is one of the first conditions of clear
legal and political thinking, and it is Hobbes's great
merit to have made this clear beyond the possibility of
misunderstanding.   No one who has grasped Hobbes's
definition can ever be misled by verbal conceits about
laws of the State which are contrary to natural right, or
the law of nature, not being binding.   All such language
is mischievous, as confusing the moral and political
grounds of positive law with its actual force.   In practice
we all know that the officers of the State cannot enter-
tain complaints that the laws enacted by the supreme
power in the State are in the complainant's opinion
unjust.   It would be impossible for government to be

---

   [1] I substitute this word for "command," as the use of that word
in a universal definition can easily be seen to be contrary to historical
fact.

carried on if they did.   Laws have to be obeyed, as between the State and the subject, not because they are reasonable, but because the State has so commanded. The laws may be, and in a wisely ordered State will be, the result of the fullest discussion which the nature of the case admits, and subsequent criticism may be allowed or even invited.   But while the laws exist they have to be obeyed.   The citizen who sets himself against the authority of the State is thereby, so far as in him lies, dissolving civil society; and this was the solid truth which Hobbes expressed in the curiously artificial form of his original covenant.   Some of Hobbes's consequences from his definition of civil law are these: The sovereign is the sole legislator in all commonwealths, and having power to make and repeal laws is not subject to the civil law.   For practical purposes it would be more useful to convert this proposition and say that the ultimate test of sovereignty in a given commonwealth is the unlimited (or better, plenary) power of legislation. If Hobbes had applied the rule in this form to England, he would have found some trouble in escaping Sir Thomas Smith's conclusion.   Then customary law depends for its force on "the will of the sovereign signified by his silence." For custom " is no longer law, than the sovereign shall be silent therein."   When it is said that law can never be against reason, this is true, but with the explanation that the commonwealth, that is, " the sovereign, which is the person of the commonwealth," is the supreme judge of what is reasonable.   The next consequence would startle the reader who took up Hobbes expect-

ing to find in him nothing but maxims of despotism.
It is that law, being a command addressed to the
subject, must be communicated in order to be effectual.
No one is answerable for breach of the law who is
incapable of entering into the original covenant of
institution or understanding its consequences; nor
is a man answerable if without his own default he
had not "the means to take notice of any particular
law."

We said above that the distinction between legality
and policy comes to us through Hobbes. The survey
of Hobbes's leading doctrines has now enabled us to see
how it comes. Hobbes defines legal sovereignty and
legal obligation with admirable strength and precision ;
but then he endeavours to swallow up policy, and to
a considerable extent even morality, in positive law.
This made it necessary to carry the work of division
further. But it was a long time before this was done.
It was Austin who completed the process in England :
and even his work was so encumbered and entangled
with irrelevant and mostly bad moral philosophy as to
spoil his philosophy of law. It would not be too much to
say that Professor Holland's *Elements of Jurisprudence* is
the first work of pure scientific jurisprudence which has
appeared in England—that is, of the general science of
law distinctly separated from the ethical part of politics.
Hobbes had indeed influence enough in England to
provoke a reaction. But its leaders applied themselves
to the wrong part of Hobbes's work. Instead of making
the doctrine of sovereignty the starting-point of fresh

criticism and construction, they endeavoured to avoid
Hobbes's consequences by devising a different sort of
original contract as the assumed foundation of society.[1]
This task we shall see undertaken by the publicists of
the eighteenth century. We shall see the original contract, seized on as a watchword by the enthusiasm of
Rousseau, grow from an arid fiction into a great and
dangerous deceit of nations. But we shall also meet
with penetrating and observant minds, which the construction of society by fiction fails to satisfy. We shall
see the dawn of the historical method in the great
Frenchman Montesquieu ; we shall see it in its full
power in the work of one greater than Montesquieu,
one of the profoundest political thinkers, and yet, by no
fault of his own, one of the least fortunate statesmen
who ever lived—our own Burke.

[1] The right kind of improvement on Hobbes was attempted by
Spinoza in his unfinished *Tractatus Politicus*. But the general aver-
sion to Spinoza's philosophy which prevailed for a century after his
death prevented this, so far as I know, from having any influence
whatever. Cp. T. H. Green, *Lectures on Political Obligation*, Lond.
1895, p. 60.

III

THE EIGHTEENTH CENTURY AND THE SOCIAL CONTRACT

THE movement in political speculation of which Locke stands at the head was the result not of a pure development of scientific ideas, but of the necessity for having a theory to justify accomplished facts. Locke's Essay on Civil Government[1] is in truth an elaborate apology for the Revolution of 1688; not ostensibly for its righteousness or policy in the particular circumstances, but for the possibility of such a proceeding being rightful in any circumstances. The partisans of James II. took their stand on a supposed indefeasible right of kings, derived from a supposed divine institution of monarchy. The doctrine of divine right has to modern eyes no sort of merit. It was not rational, it was not ingenious, it was not even ancient. A certain sanctity had indeed attached to kings from time immemorial. But this belonged to the office, not to the person apart from the office. Because the man had a kind of sacred character while he was king, it by no means followed that being once made king he could not be unmade, or was entitled

---

[1] I have contributed a fuller discussion of Locke's theory of the State to vol. i. of the *Proceedings* of the British Academy, Lond. 1905.

to retain and exercise the office without conditions. The notion of the office itself being something above human disposition and jurisdiction had been accepted only in the current century. Still, absurd as it was, it was fortified by a great show of respectable authority. It had taken root in many minds, and become a motive or a stumbling-block in many good men's consciences. The Whigs needed an antidote, and Locke found one in his modified version of the original compact. Hooker had to some extent prepared the way. Long before his time Fortescue, and probably others, had, in a confused fashion, represented the English constitution as in some way founded on the deliberate assent of the original founders of the Commonwealth. In the first book of Hooker's treatise of the Laws of Ecclesiastical Polity the conception takes a distinct shape. The plainer-spoken doctrine of the natural state of war which afterwards gave so much offence in Hobbes is virtually foreshadowed in Hooker's paragraph on the condition of men without civil government : and the origin of government is in express terms referred to "deliberate advice, consultation, and composition between men." Hooker adds his opinion that there is "no impossibility in nature considered by itself, but that men might have lived without any public regiment"; a phrase which looks like a wilful contradiction of Aristotle's axiom, though, considering the respect with which Hooker

---

[1] In its origin it seems to have been an anti-papal doctrine intended to fortify the authority of secular princes against the claims of the Holy See: Figgis, *The Divine Right of Kings*, Cambridge, 2nd edition, 1914.

constantly cites Aristotle, it is difficult to believe that it was in fact so meant. We may also discover both here and in the unfinished eighth book a nascent theory of sovereignty, but it is nascent at most. Had the divine to whom the name of Judicious was eminently applied by the next generation worked out anything definite in this direction, it would probably have shown more regard for the historical conditions of English politics and the practical possibilities of government than the heroic method of Hobbes.

Locke sets to work to cast the ideas of Hooker (whom he expressly cites) into a better defined form. His definition of political power is curiously lumbering and loaded with qualifications, as if he were afraid of giving a handle to despotism. He begins with a state of nature, but he conceives of it otherwise than Hobbes. The mark of the state of nature is the "want of a common judge with authority"; but men in this state are not in absolute anarchy. They are subject to the law of reason, which "teaches all mankind, who will but consult it, that being all equal and independent, no one ought to harm another in his life, health, liberty, or possessions." As there are no adequate means of enforcing that law, their peace is precarious; nevertheless an actual state of war arises only when some one, not having the law of reason before his eyes, puts himself out of its protection by offering violence to others. Locke has an answer in due form to the question by what right the others may resist and even kill the offender. In the state of nature every one alike has the executive power of the law of nature; and this power is even in modern societies the only justification for the exercise of sovereignty over aliens within the territorial dominion of a State. One would here expect Locke to come at once to the original compact; but he is too wary for this. He will first establish as much private right as he can; and he argues with much ingenuity for a natural right of property which is altogether antecedent to government. Every man is said to have "a property in his own person,"[1] and this is extended to things which he has changed from their natural state by doing work upon them, or in Locke's phrase, "hath mixed his labour with." Conflict of interests is foreseen, and is accordingly forestalled by the rule of nature that the right of property is limited by capacity of enjoyment, or at any rate of permanent safe custody. After some preliminary discussion of the constitution of the family we come at length to political society, which is described in a curiously indecisive manner. Man "hath by nature a power not only to preserve his property, that is, his life, liberty, and estate, against the injuries and attempts of other men, but to judge of and punish the breach of that law" (*i.e.* the law of nature) "in others. . . . But because no political society can be, nor subsist without having in itself the power to preserve the property, and in order thereunto, punish the offences of all of that society; there, and there only, is political society, where every one of the

---

[1] Ulpian's contrary opinion "dominus membrorum suorum nemo videtur" (D. ix. 2, ad. leg. Aquil. 13) is more acceptable both to modern lawyers and to modern philosophers.

members hath quitted this natural power, and resigned it up into the hands of the community in all cases that exclude him not from appealing for protection to the law established by it. And thus all private judgment of every particular member being excluded, the community comes to be umpire by settled standing rules, indifferent and the same to all parties." Every man gives up his actual power to the community, not to a sovereign ruler as with Hobbes; and he gives it up not absolutely, but for particular and limited purposes. Whoever joins an existing commonwealth becomes a party to the original contract on which it rests by accepting the benefit of it, and is as much bound as if he had been present and assisting at the first institution. Locke then proves (no doubt as against Hobbes) that an absolute monarchy is not a civil society at all, for an absolute monarch, being no "common judge with authority" to decide between himself and his subjects, is really in the state of nature with regard to them. When a political society is formed, the right of a majority to be the ultimate source of power is deduced as a practical necessity. Without such right the commonwealth could not act as one body at all. And for this Locke appeals to actual usage : "We see that in assemblies empowered to act by positive laws, where no number is set by that positive law which empowers them, the act of the majority passes for the act of the whole, and of course determines, as having by the law of nature and reason the power of the whole."

Political society, then, is in Locke's theory consti-
tuted by the compact of its original members, a compact
renewed from generation to generation in the person of
every citizen when he comes to an age of discretion to
choose his allegiance.   If he chooses, as in the vast
majority of cases he does, to go on living in the State
where he was brought up, he thereby becomes a party to
its Constitution, and authorises its sovereignty over him
But the sovereignty of the society is not absolute.   It is
limited to the ends for which it was conferred; the
State is like a corporate joint-stock company, whose
operations cannot lawfully extend beyond the purposes
for which it was incorporated.   Men have established
governments not to control their lives altogether, but
"for the mutual preservation of their lives, liberties,
and estates." Forms of government may be and are
various, but the fundamental principles are the same.
The legislative power is supreme, and all members of
the State owe obedience to it; but its authority is not
arbitrary.   First, it must be exercised as it was given,
for the good of the subjects.   Secondly, it must dispense
justice by standing laws and authorised judges; for
under irregular arbitrary power the subjects would be
worse off than in the state of nature.   Thirdly, no man
can be deprived of any part of his property without his
own consent, given either in person or by his representatives ; or as Locke more correctly puts it in
summing up, "they must not raise taxes on the property
of the people, without the consent of the people, given by
themselves or their deputies."   Fourthly, the legislature

cannot transfer its powers to any other person or body. These are organic maxims of government which (so far as one can make sure of Locke's meaning) cannot be dispensed with by any power whatever. Excellent maxims they are, but we should now say that they are rules of political expediency, not limits to the legal capacity of the authority by whom laws themselves are made; unless indeed they are expressed in a formal constitution which the ordinary legislature cannot alter, but Locke does not consider any such case.

Locke is aware, it should be said, of the objection that the state of nature is an unproved and improbable assumption, and the original contract, therefore, no better than a fiction. He seriously endeavours to deal with it, though the attempt cannot be pronounced successful. The state of nature, he says, is exhibited as a thing really existing in modern times by the relation of independent States to one another. As to the want of evidence that it was the primeval state of mankind in general, he says that the very obscurity of all early records and absence of positive knowledge leave the ground all the more clear for any probable hypothesis of the origin of society.

Subject to these conditions, which in some points curiously resemble those imposed on sovereignty by Bodin, Locke is quite clear that, " whilst the government subsists, the legislative is the supreme power ; for what can give laws to another, must needs be superior to him." But its authority is not indefeasible : " being only a fiduciary power to act for certain ends," it may be forfeited by misuse.   Under every form of government the community retains a supreme power of self-preservation, a power which, underlying all positive institutions, and not being bound to any of them, " can never take place till the government be dissolved." Hobbes would say that this alleged power is merely a specious name for the *de facto* possibility of a successful rebellion, followed by a return to the natural state of war, in other words for that anarchy which is to be avoided at all costs. Further on Locke, as if to meet this objection, is at no small pains to show that the dissolution of governments is to be distinguished from that of societies.   " Where the society is dissolved, the government cannot remain ; " but governments may be altered or dissolved from within, and the society not be destroyed.   Locke seems to regard the original agreement as having two stages.   First, people agree to live in a commonwealth ; next, that the institutions of their particular commonwealth shall have this or that form and in the form so chosen shall be observed.[1]   So far as the agreement concerns the establishment of a community in general, it is perpetual and irrevocable ; so far as it places authority in the hands of a dynasty or an assembly, it is subject to revision whenever organic change is demanded by the common good.   Locke illustrates his position by cases hypothetical in terms, but having

[1] *Pactum unionis* and *pactum subiectionis* in the language of Continental publicists. It is the second or auxiliary compact that is renewed in every member's person. Locke does not make it very clear whether he postulates a double compact, but on the whole he seems to do so.

a transparent reference to the English Constitution and the Revolution of 1688. He never distinctly faces the question whether a change of government can take place within the limits of positive law. This omission seems remarkable when we remember that the Convention Parliament, " lawfully, fully, and freely representing all the estates of the people of this realm," had expressed itself in the affirmative in sufficiently plain terms. It is impossible to read the Bill of Rights carefully without seeing that its framers were convinced not only of the justice and policy but of the strict legality of their proceedings, though it is far from certain that they were right on this point. Technical difficulties were felt as to the exact manner in which James II. had legally ceased to be king. But the Revolution was conducted throughout as a reformation within the law, nay, as a restoration of the law, not as a breaking of legal bonds which had become intolerable. It was Locke's way, however, to swallow up legality in policy almost as much as Hobbes had swallowed up policy in legality.

At one point Locke comes down, as against Hobbes, on the hard bottom of facts, and does it with great effect. He expects the objection that " this hypothesis " (of the possible forfeiture of political power) "lays a ferment for frequent rebellion." And he answers, " No more than any other hypothesis; for when the people are made miserable, and find themselves exposed to the ill-usage of arbitrary power, cry up their governors as much as you will, for sons of Jupiter; let them be sacred or divine, descended or authorised from heaven, give them out for whom or what you please, the same will happen." The preaching of Hobbes's irrevocable covenant of sovereignty, or Filmer's patriarchal title of kings deduced from Adam, will not make people endure a government that is in fact unendurable. It is by no means clear that Hobbes was not ready to say it would; it is clear, at any rate, from divers passages in his *Leviathan* and elsewhere, that he set an exaggerated value upon the influence of political theories propagated under colour of civil or ecclesiastical authority. He seems to have thought the bulk of men would believe whatever their superiors told them, even when their own obvious interests were concerned, and the sovereign might make them believe what he pleased if he took care to allow no superior but himself.

For the rest, the hesitations and half-truths of Locke and his followers are partly to be accounted for by the practical conditions of their work. They dared not say distinctly that the king of England was not sovereign in the political sense of sovereignty. Locke says, for example, that " in some commonwealths, where the legislative is not always in being, and the executive is vested in a single person, who has also a share in the legislative, there that single person in a very tolerable sense may also be called supreme." Besides this, Locke was evidently afraid on principle of over-definition. He is nowhere so precise on the supreme authority of Parliament (for the English Parliament is constantly in his mind when he speaks of the " legislative ") as Sir

Thomas Smith a century before him. On prerogative, again, he is not so plain-spoken or exact as Selden had been. Selden, like a clear-headed lawyer, said there was no mystery at all. Prerogative is the law which peculiarly concerns the Crown, and is not different in kind from any other branch of law.[1] With Locke there is still a shadow of mystery about it. Prerogative is a vague and extraordinary discretion, limited, like the legislative power itself, by the rule that it must be employed in good faith for the public advantage.

The plastic fiction of the original contract had been used by Hobbes to generate the absolute power of his *Leviathan*, and by Locke to show that a moderate constitutional government not merely was justified by the law of nature, but was the only government so justified. It remained for Rousseau to employ the same fiction for purposes which Hobbes would have thought the very madness of anarchy, and at which Locke would have been appalled. Locke's propositions, as Lord Morley has pointed out, are guarded by practical reserve on all sides, and are as far as possible from being portable and universal dogmas. Rousseau was more popular than Locke, and more dogmatic than Hobbes. The result was that the *Contrat Social* became one of the most successful and fatal of political impostures.[2]

[1] Selden, *Table-talk*, *s.v.* Prerogative.
[2] It contains incidentally the ambiguous maxim : " La guerre n'est point une relation d'homme à homme, mais une relation d'état à état," which contains some truth, but as a universal proposition is far too wide. For fuller statement see W. A. Dunning, " Rousseau's Political Theories," *Pol. Sci. Quarterly*, September 1909.

Rousseau's [1] social contract is distinguished from that of other speculators in purporting to create a common and sovereign power, and yet leave every contracting party as free as he was before, and owing obedience only to himself. Every man gives up himself and his individual rights as fully as in Hobbes's covenant. But the surrender is to the whole society, not to a sovereign. " Chacun se donnant a tous ne se donne à personne." The terms of the contract (for Rousseau knows all about the terms) are as follows :—" Each of us puts his person and faculties in a common stock under the sovereign direction of the general will; and we receive [2] every member as an inseparable part of the whole." Every member is called *citizen* as having a share in the sovereignty, *subject* as owing obedience to the laws made by the State. Whoever refuses to obey the general will is to be compelled by the whole body to obey it: " which is as much as to say that he will be compelled to be free "—an ominous phrase. The sovereign power thus created is spoken of in a tone which Hobbes could not surpass. It is inalienable, indivisible, and, it would seem, infallible, if you can only get the " general will " truly expressed. The sovereign is bound to be just in the sense of having no respect of persons. Law is defined by the one mark of generality, so that the choice of a king or a dynasty cannot be a legislative act. A definition by which the Bill of Rights is partly a law and partly not, and the Act of Settlement is not one

[1] See now Vaughan's critical edition of his political writings, 1916.
[2] " Recevons en corps."

at all, does not particularly commend itself to the English student of politics. Rousseau's object is apparently to reconcile Hobbes's dictum that no law can be unjust, which he adopts, with his own definition of the justice required in the sovereign. Further, no power in the State can be sovereign. The legislator is not sovereign, but the organ and servant of the sovereign community. The government is not the sovereign, but a mediator between the community in its corporate and sovereign capacity and its individual members as subjects. As the government cannot legislate, so the sovereign cannot govern directly. But the tendency of governments is to aim at usurping sovereignty ; sooner or later the ruler subjugates the sovereign, and the fundamental pact of society is broken. This is the inherent weakness of all commonwealths, by which they ultimately perish. The political as well as the natural body is on the way to death from the moment it begins to live.

Rousseau does not fail to see that the complete exercise of sovereign power, according to his notion of it, is impossible ; for how are the sovereign people all to come together ? His answer is that modern States are a great deal too large : he would restore the independent Greek city, or what he supposed it to be. When the people are assembled every citizen is equally a magistrate, and all government is in abeyance. Representative government, where it exists, is only a makeshift ; deputies of the people cannot really represent its power, they can be only limited agents whose acts need ratification. English liberty is an illusion ; for the English people is the slave of the Parliament it makes. Political representation is indeed no better than a rag of feudal iniquity. Thus for want of a proper declaration of the "general will" there is hardly a nation on earth which possesses laws in any proper sense. But then, how to unite the just and true sovereignty of the people with the size and defensive resources of the modern State? Rousseau promised to deal at large with this question, but did not perform his promise in the *Contrat Social*, or any other published writing.[1] Apparently his plan would have been the establishment of some sort of federal government for purposes of external policy. The federal constitution of Switzerland, though in his time a very imperfect one, would have no doubt fur- nished a good part of his matter for this head.

The social contract had sometimes been represented as including, or identical with, a contract between the king or other ruler and the people. Rousseau formally repudiates this. Government is created in his view, not by contract, but by an act of sovereignty. The sup- posed contract, he says (truly enough, but the remark comes strangely from him), would be not civil but merely natural, and would be under the sanction of no common authority. There is only one contract, the original contract of society; this leaves no room for any other, for the community has acquired by it all the rights of its individual members.[2] So confident is Rousseau in the

[1] It is stated that he left materials on this subject which were destroyed from political scruples. Their custodian need not have feared to publish them. It would have been difficult to add to the mischief wrought by the *Contrat Social* without their aid.

[2] In technical terms, the original *pactum unionis* created a supreme power and a subsequent *pactum subiectionis* is needless.

indefeasible rights of the sovereign people that he seems to approve of delegations of authority which constitutional writers like Locke thought dangerous and unwarrantable. He speaks with equanimity of a dictatorship. In the days of the Committee of Public Safety the Jacobin governors of France more than acted up to his principles. One more great difficulty remained about the exercise of the sovereign people's rights. Rousseau had of course, like all other absolute theorists on government, to make out why a dissenting citizen should be bound by the will of the majority. This he does in a fashion both more sophistical and more clumsy than Locke's. Locke indeed is frank enough in his appeal to practical convenience on this point.

Thus much for a rapid sketch of Rousseau's political system, of which the historical importance is that it is in great measure answerable for the Declaration of the Rights of Man.[1] This Declaration (which belongs to the earliest stage of the Revolution) carries the confusion of legal right and political expediency, and the enunciation of pompous platitudes under qualifications so wide as to make them illusory, to a pitch seldom, if ever, equalled in any other political document. The birth of all men free and with equal rights, the collective sovereignty of the nation, and the " volonté générale "

[1] The full text of this document (which most historians strangely neglect) is given in Henri Martin's *Histoire de la France depuis* 1789, vol. i. p. 78. It has, however, lost most of its importance in modern French politics, as the learned French translator of the present work has pointed out in his note here.

which positive laws express, are taken straight from Rousseau. It would be unjust to deny all merit to the Declaration. The 7th, 8th, and 9th articles express, in language fairly free from objection, important maxims of legislation and administrative jurisprudence. But so far as the Declaration embodies a political theory, it is a standing warning to nations and states-men not to commit themselves to formulas. The original contract between king and people had been much talked of at Westminster in the debates on the abdication of James II.; but happily we escaped having it embodied in the Bill of Rights. The effect of the Principles of 1789, as the Declaration of the Rights of Man is often called, has been to hinder and prevent the development of politics in France, in practice as well as in theory, to an almost incalculable extent.

While Rousseau's *Contrat Social* was almost fresh from the press, Blackstone was handling Locke's principles in England after quite another fashion. If we dismiss from our minds Bentham's fervid criticism, and approach Blackstone in an unprejudiced mood, we shall find that he not only was faithful to his lights, but materially improved on Locke in more than one point.[1] For one thing, he distinctly refuses to believe

[1] It is easy for us now to make light of Blackstone's constitutional theory. Two things, I conceive, ought to be remembered in fairness to him. (1) Blackstone wrote as a lawyer; and, as far as positive law goes, a hopeless deadlock was and is quite possible in the working of the English Constitution as it stood in his time and stood till 1911. (2) The distribution of real political power between the Crown and the two Houses of Parliament was still undefined at the date of Blackstone's description. We now say that political power, as distinct from legal sovereignty, is in the last resort with the majority of the House of Commons. Blackstone not only would not but could not have said so

in the state of nature as an historical fact, and thereby avoids a difficulty which Locke had palliated rather than met by ingenious but weak excuses. " Society had not its formal beginning from any convention of individuals." Blackstone treats the family as the unit of society, and reduces the original contract, though he does not abandon the term, to the fact that men hold together in society because they cannot help it. On the doctrine of sovereignty, again, he is much clearer than Locke. In all forms of government " there is and must be a supreme, irresistible, absolute, uncontrolled authority, in which the *jura summa imperii* or the rights of sovereignty reside." And, going back to Sir Thomas Smith's doctrine, he affirms, as against Locke's vague reservations, that in England this authority belongs to Parliament, and there is no legal possibility of looking further. "What the parliament doth, no authority upon earth can undo." The separation of law from policy is still far from complete, but Blackstone is nearer to the true state of the facts than either Hobbes or Locke.

Rousseau and Blackstone have been taken out of their order in time for the convenience of bringing into one view the social contract in its various forms. Meantime the doctrine had not escaped criticism on its native soil. Hume, taking a double pleasure, we may be sure, in dissecting a philosophical fallacy which was almost a Whig article of faith, exposed its hollowness in such fashion as really left nothing more to be said. But Hume was a destroyer, not a rebuilder. He had nothing to put in the place of the beloved fiction, which accordingly went on living in political commonplace, as Leslie Stephen has said, long after the brains were out. His own political conceptions were poor and mechanical, and his idea of a perfect commonwealth is one of the most barren and least pleasing exercises of political imagination ever produced. It was a Frenchman who supplied beforehand, if his countrymen would have appreciated it, an antidote to Rousseau's fictions. Montesquieu,[1] with all his faults and irregularities, is the father of modern historical research. His information was often crude and imperfect, his inferences often hasty, and his judgment often misdirected. Yet he held fast to the great truth that serious politics cannot be constructed in the air by playing with imaginary men of no particular race or country, and building them into arbitrary combinations, as a child builds castles with wooden bricks. He applied himself to study political institutions as belonging to societies of definite historical types, and determined by historical conditions. One may remember with a certain pride that he was a member of our own Royal Society, which thus early recognised in his person that the questions of politics as well as of physics may be treated in a scientific spirit, so as to give a truly scientific character to the inquirer's work.

Montesquieu's plan included two ideas, which were

[1] See now M. Albert Sorel's monograph *Montesquieu*, Paris, 1887, and cp. Sir Courtenay Ilbert's Romanes lecture on Montesquieu, Oxford, 1904. Montesquieu's great work was published anonymously at Geneva in 1748, and officially admitted to circulate in France only two years later. An Edinburgh edition of 1750 was still anonymous.

brilliant in themselves and quite out of the common course of the publicists of the time. He aimed at constructing a comparative theory of legislation and institutions adapted to the political needs of different forms of government, and a comparative theory of politics and law based on wide observation of the actual systems of different lands and ages. In the first branch of this design Machiavelli had, after a sort, been before him, but in a limited field and for a special purpose. The second was entirely new. We have already said that the execution was not equal to the conception. The means did not exist for making it so. Few books are so unfit to be judged by extracts or cursory inspection as the *Esprit des Lois*. There are many chapters in it which might have come from a mere gossiping collector of traveller's tales. Nor is Montesquieu by any means always happy in his reflections. He was above many of the illusions of his time, but he could not escape the besetting temptation of the eighteenth century to regard men as more rational than they are. Thus we find him assigning conjectural reasons of State policy for all kinds of barbarous customs, more or less correctly reported by Jesuit missionaries and others. He rightly saw that customs which appear to us foolish or monstrous do not exist without any reason at all. He no less rightly saw that the institutions of a society depend on its particular conditions, and must be studied in connection with them ; but in counting the conditions he left out the men themselves. He did not see that to understand a civil society widely differing from our own

we must first get some knowledge of the ancestral habits
and character of its members, and of the stage they
have reached in general culture.   In one word, he
stopped short of discovering that institutions are an
affair of race as well as of circumstances ; [1] not far short,
for he went a considerable way in the application of
physiology to politics.   It is not so much that Montesquieu neglects race as that he exaggerates the
modifying effect of external conditions.   And we also
find his historical method, imperfect as it was, preserving
him from a great many current mistakes.   For example,
he completely sees through the rose-coloured accounts
of the Chinese empire which were the common stock of
eighteenth-century moralists and even of Voltaire, and
this because he has taken the trouble to study the facts
as a whole.

Again, Montesquieu's remarks on England, of which
he has a good many (though sometimes thinly disguised,
like Locke's, in the form of suppositions), are by no
means free from mistakes ; but they show on the whole
a wonderful insight into the effectual forces of English
policy, and what is more, into English character. [2]   It is
needless to say much of his general enlightenment and
robustness of mind.   A writer who in the middle of the

[1] M. Sorel says, "L'erreur de Montesquieu n'est pas d'avoir recherché
l'influence de ces éléments [l'air, le sol, le pays, la race], c'est de n'en
avoir considéré qu'un seul et de ne l'avoir considéré qu'avec des données
très incomplètes."

[2] On some points of English foreign and colonial policy Montesquieu, though to some extent he is describing facts already observed,
is almost prophetic.—Esp. des Lois, book xix. c. 27.   Sorel justly
called attention to the scientific prevision displayed in this chapter.

eighteenth century could suggest, though in an ironical passage, an international convention against the slave trade, needs no further commendation. Once more, he meets with rare straightforwardness the ancient objection to popular government—that the people at large are not competent in politics. It is not to be expected, says Montesquieu, that they should be competent, nor does it much matter. The main thing is that they should be interested. Experience and discussion must be trusted to make error find its level. "Dans une nation libre, il est très-souvent indifférent que les particuliers raisonnent bien ou mal; il suffit qu'ils raisonnent : de là sort la liberté, qui garantit des effets de ces mêmes raisonnements."

Montesquieu was vastly honoured in his own country, but not much attended to for any practical purpose. In so far as the politicians of the Revolution did make any use of Montesquieu, it was to follow and exaggerate his errors. He was much better understood in England, and has even been called the spiritual father of Blackstone.[1] But there was barely time for his work, first published in 1748, to have much influence on Blackstone's, which was put into shape as a course of lectures[2] at Oxford as early as 1753. Our own Burke fared even worse than Montesquieu; he had the melancholy satisfaction of seeing his wisest counsels neglected, and seeing the neglect of them followed by the evils he predicted;

[1] Sorel, p. 143 ; "Blackstone procède de lui."
[2] Not Vinerian lectures : the Vinerian chair was established, and Blackstone became the first Professor, only in 1758.

and when at last he was taken into favour it was because his political reason fell in for once with the blind passions of those who had denounced him as a renegade.

Just now I said that Montesquieu was a difficult author to give a fair representation of in any summary manner. For, though he professes to be systematic, he is too discursive and unequal to be judged of in abridgment. Neither will an epitome of the matter serve much for knowledge of his real import, since his merit is often far more in the disposition and handling than in the matter itself. With Burke the difficulty is yet greater ; he is full of ideas more instructive than other men's systems, but they are so admirably woven into the discussion of particular and actual questions that they refuse to be torn out as examples of him. They proceed from a settled way of thinking, but are nowhere reduced into a collected argument. A light of great wisdom shines in almost everything of Burke's making, but it is a diffused light, of which the focus is not revealed but only conjectured. This is in the first place due to the manner of Burke's life and to the occasions of his activity ; but it is also connected with the nature of his thought itself. We may be pretty sure that Burke would under no conditions have constructed a formal theory of politics. He mistrusted formalism even to excess, and was never so happy as when he used the most splendid power of political reasoning ever exhibited in English oratory to denounce the danger of reasoning overmuch. He was not afraid to say that he feared definitions. " Metaphysics cannot live without

definitions, but prudence is cautious how she defines."
He declared himself "resolved not to be wise beyond
what is written in the legislative record and practice."
Not only is Burke not formally complete as a political
teacher, but if we look for formal consistency in him we
shall not find it. When he is denouncing the monstrous
penal laws of Ireland he sets the conventional value of
positive laws as low as possible. Curiously anticipating
in one point almost the very language of the greatest
master of the modern historical school, Burke says that
"as a law directed against the mass of the nation has
not the nature of a reasonable institution, so neither has
it the authority : *for in all forms of government the
people is the true legislator* ;[1] and whether the immediate
and instrumental cause of the law be a single person or
many, the remote and efficient cause is the consent of
the people, either actual or implied; and such consent
is absolutely essential to its validity." Even the whole
people "have no right to make a law prejudicial to the
whole community." When the same Burke is com-
bating the Declaration of the Rights of Man he speaks
of legal power in a strangely different tone. In the
Tracts on the Popery Laws Hobbes is just mentioned as
having broached a monstrous doctrine ; in the *Reflections
on the French Revolution* we catch for a moment the
ring of Hobbes's doctrine almost in Hobbes's own words.
"If civil society be the offspring of convention that
convention must be its law;" no person can claim any
right inconsistent with it. "That he may obtain justice

[1] Compare Savigny's "Das Gesetz ist das Organ des Volksrechts."

he gives up his right of determining what it is in points the most essential to him. That he may secure some liberty he makes a surrender in trust of the whole of it." Government is a thing apart from natural rights ; it is contrived to provide for men's wants and to restrain their passions, which " can only be done *by a power out of themselves*"—Hobbes's " common power to keep them in awe." And for the moment we think Burke is ready to fall down and worship the Leviathan if Leviathan will put a sword in his hand to smite the Jacobins with.

Yet it is the same Burke who speaks in both places, and really with the same voice. His anger against Protestant oppression in Ireland and Jacobin violence in France comes from one and the same root. His constant purpose, whether in the affairs of Ireland, of England, or of France, is to appeal to experience against dogmatism. He will have for the guide of politics neither the bare letter of positive institutions nor bare deduction from universal propositions, but a rule of equity and utility founded on and preserving the rights and liberties which exist. He will treat politics as an experimental science, not a scheme of *à priori* demonstration. Once he was challenged with substantial defection from his own principles. His *Reflections on the French Revolution* were said to be repugnant to his former public life. The result was the *Appeal from the New to the Old Whigs*, in which, by dint of criticising the Jacobin theory of society, Burke is brought nearer than in any other of his works to an explicit statement of his own.

We are bidden, he says, in the name of the supreme authority of the people to recognise as a matter, not of extraordinary necessity, but of common right, an unlimited power of changing the foundations of government. What are the people? "A number of vague, loose individuals"—the imaginary parties to the social contract—are not a people, neither can they make themselves one off-hand by convention. A "multitude told by heads" is no more a people after it has been told than before. The corporate unity of a people is artificial indeed; but art is long, and for that very reason a nation is easier unmade than made. And how is the supreme authority of the people exercised? By the will of a majority. But what power has the majority to bind the rest? Again an artificial power, nay, a most artificial power. First there is a fiction to make one corporate person of many men; then another fiction, "one of the most violent fictions of positive law," to enable a majority to act as this one person. And on these artificial and judicial conceptions, confusing, as Burke says, judicial with civil principles, the French revolutionary speculators would rest the authority of positive law itself. Whether a majority shall have power to decide, in what cases, and what majority, is an affair of convention. These people have no right, on their own principles, to exercise any of the authorities of a State. If "prescription and long possession form no title to property," what better claim have they than a horde of brigands or squatters to the territory called France? Civil society will not come by counting of

heads; it is a social organism and a social discipline.
And if it is artificial in its perfection, yet it is more
truly a state of nature "than a savage and incoherent
mode of life," or rather it is this because it is artificial,
for "art is man's nature." Such is the substance of
Burke's comment on the fundamental axiom of Aristotle.
Man is born to be a citizen in that he comes into an
existing social order, and is attached to it by duties of
others to himself and himself to others, which are not,
and cannot be, of his own making. He does not come
into the world as an unrelated unit and acquire by some
convention a fantastic title to some hundred-thousandth
undivided part of the indivisible sovereignty of the
people.

Never was there a more complete tearing to pieces
and trampling underfoot of political sophistries. The
Contrat Social is reduced in Burke's powerful hands to
what he had elsewhere called it—"chaff and rags and
paltry blurred shreds of paper about the rights of man."
It seems hardly possible that such a critic should fall
into sophistries himself; but he thought little of being
guarded, and more than once he stumbles. Regarding
political science as above all things experimental and
practical he took up, as he tells us himself, whatever
point he thought most in need of defence, and urged his
case without qualification of the matter, and without
thinking much of other sides. Thus we find in him
forms of statement and objection which in a lesser man
we should call obtuse. Believing, as he justly did, in
the respect due to the continuity of the present with

the past, and to associations which cannot be replaced, he looked on the analysis of the ultimate forces of society as a kind of sacrilege. He could see no practical security for the British Constitution if the French principles of 1789 were to be held tolerable even in speculation. The security of sympathisers with the revolution—those who profess to be peaceable ones—"amounts in reality to nothing more than this, that the difference between their republican system and the British limited monarchy is not worth a civil war." And this is called by Burke "the poorest defensive principle that ever was infused into the mind of man against the attempts of those who will enterprise." As if in the last resort any frame of society whatever had any other defensive principle, or as if any stronger were conceivable. Hobbes could find no firmer ground to set under the feet of the Leviathan. The vast majority of men adhere to their established institutions, not because they admire them, not even because of any positive prejudice in their favour, but because they dread the unknown. They cling to any tolerable certainty for certainty and custom's sake, and when they break loose from their accustomed order it is a vehement presumption that their present state is not only imperfect but intolerable. When it comes to that point no prescriptive majesty of the ancient order will help it, not though the voice of a Burke were there to defend it. In 1832 a large part of the English people were of opinion that the difference between an unreformed and a reformed Parliament *was* worth a civil war; and it was

the knowledge of their opinion and of their readiness
in extremity to act on it that then narrowly saved the
State.   Burke failed to see this in the case of the
French Revolution, and therefore was violent and one-
sided.   Shallow or false he could not be ; stripped of
their rhetorical exaggerations, or often even with them,
his charges were mostly true, and his foresight of the
course of events was marvellously fulfilled.   In 1789,
and even later, many good people, both in Paris and
London, were dreaming of a happy and peaceful change
from the old French monarchy to some new version of
the British Constitution.   Burke warned them from the
first that at all events they would not see *that*, and he
was terribly in the right.

After Burke it was impossible for any one in
England to set up the Social Contract again, either in
Rousseau's or in Locke's form, for any effectual purpose
There is another distinct contribution both to political
science and to exactness of reasoning in practical
politics, which I think we may ascribe to him : the
separation of expediency from legality.   It might be
difficult to show in his writings any full and formal
enunciation of this ; but it is the whole burden of his
great speeches and letters on the American War.
Englishmen were declaiming on the right of the British
Parliament to tax the colonists.   Burke told them the
abstract right might be what it would, but they were
fighting against justice, convenience, and human nature,
and for the sake of their abstract right were making a
breach in the dominions of the British Crown.   The
event signally and unhappily showed his wisdom.

Burke, however, was too great for his generation. He restored history to its place in politics, but, like some of the greatest thinkers in pure philosophy, he left no disciples. The formal development of political science in the nineteenth century is not traced through him, but was taken up in England from a wholly different side, and on the Continent by an independent impulse, though in a spirit, and sometimes even in a form, which have more affinities with Burke than with any other Englishman.

IV

MODERN THEORIES OF SOVEREIGNTY AND LEGISLATION

WE have now come down to the beginning of the nine-teenth century, a date from which the development of political speculation becomes too vast and multifarious to be dealt with on a uniform scale in such a summary sketch as the present. A choice must of necessity be made among the various branches of the subject. An attempt to exhibit their general character is made in the accompanying tables. In one group we have the oldest branch of political science, the general theory of the State and its possible forms. This has received much additional definition at the hands of modern authors, and in England in particular the doctrine of sovereignty has been found inadequate, like all dogmatic formulas, to account for complex facts. In a second group comes the study of particular institutions and the action of the State for particular purposes, which may be called as a whole the theory of government. Here seems to be the fittest place for the question of what things ought to be dealt with by the State and what left alone, a question associated with sundry terms and phrases such as *laissez faire*, limits of the State, individual liberty. Then a more technical branch of the subject has to do with the State in its legal aspect, in other words with the method, form, and application of positive law. This may be named the theory of legislation in a wide sense, and legal science as specially understood by lawyers may be regarded in the logical order as an offshoot from it, though the shoot is considerably larger than the parent stem, and, in the historical order, much older. Lastly, the State is personified for the purpose of external action, and regarded as having duties towards other States and claims upon them. A systematic doctrine of these duties and rights is given by the law of nations and the speculative theories which profess to support or account for it. This division, except as to the last branch, is to a great extent not really a division of different subjects, but a distinction of the forms and relations under which the same subjects are presented ; neither does it attempt exact analysis, which indeed the nature of the matter hardly admits. But it may serve to show the range and variety of modern political science.

THEORETICAL POLITICS.	APPLIED POLITICS.
A. THEORY OF THE STATE.	A. THE STATE.
Origin of Polity.	Existing forms of govern-ment.
a. Historical.	
b. Rational.	Confederations and Federal States.
Constitution.	
Classification of forms of government.	Independence.
	Protectorates and extra-territorial jurisdiction.
Political Sovereignty.	

THEORETICAL POLITICS.	APPLIED POLITICS.

B. THEORY OF GOVERNMENT.
Forms of institutions.
    Representative and Ministerial Government.
    Executive Departments.
      Defence and Order.
      Revenue and Taxation.
      Wealth of Nations.
Province and Limits of Positive Law.
	B. GOVERNMENT.
	Constitutional Law and Usage.
	Parliamentary Systems.
	Cabinet and Ministerial Responsibility.
	Administrative Constitutions.
	Army, Navy, Police.
	Currency, Budget, Trade.
	State regulation or non-interference.

C. THEORY OF LEGISLATION. Objects of Legislation. General Character and Divisions of Positive Law (Philosophy of Law or General Jurisprudence). Method and Sanction of Laws. Interpretation and Administration. Language and Style (Mechanics of Law-making).	**C. LAWS AND LEGISLATION.** Legislative Procedure. (Embodiment of theory in legislative forms : memorandum, *exposé des motifs*, etc.) Parliamentary drafting. Jurisprudence of particular States. Courts of Justice and their machinery. Judicial precedents and authority.
D. THEORY OF THE STATE AS ARTIFICIAL PERSON. Relation to other States and bodies of men. International Law.	**D. THE STATE PERSONIFIED.** Diplomacy, Peace and War. Conferences, Treaties and Conventions. International agreements for furtherance of justice, commerce, communications, etc

It seems natural to choose for closer inspection such

topics as, being in themselves important, have been more than others handled by English writers and connected with practical questions of legislation and policy. Dismissing international law, which otherwise answers this description, as too technical and standing too much apart, we find political sovereignty and the limits of State intervention to be topics of the desired kind. On these English literature, if not abundant, can make a fair show, and on one or other of them a great part of modern English political discussion has turned, so far as it has involved speculative ideas at all. It will therefore be convenient to mention particularly what has been done by English writers on these subjects, marking in other directions only the most general characters of the different modern schools of political theory. In a fuller exposition it would be proper to give some special attention to theories of the State presented by philosophers in organic connexion with their general view of the universe, and the influence of such theories, especially the Hegelian, on modern publicists who were not professed philosophers. But this cannot be attempted here.[1]

There is no doubt who has the first claim upon us. It was Bentham who, after the interval of a century, took up the theory of sovereignty where Hobbes had left it, and showed it to be capable of a reasonable interpretation, and fruitful of practical consequences.

[1] So far as I know, the only complete work of the kind recently published in English is Mr. Bernard Bosanquet's *Philosophical Theory of the State* (1899). T. H. Green's posthumous lectures on Political Obligation should also be consulted.

His *Fragment on Government*, a short book, but containing all his leading ideas, appeared in 1776. Not only the ideas are there, but they are much better expressed than in Bentham's own later versions of them. No man ever laboured more assiduously than Bentham in his old age to make the outward form of his thoughts repulsive or ridiculous to the public. Happily the thoughts have now become common property, and the later volumes of Bentham's collected works may repose undisturbed, save by any curious student of the follies of great men who may have the patience to see what violence can be done to the English language by a philosopher under the dominion of his own inventions. The *Fragment* is a merciless criticism on the introductory part of Blackstone's Commentaries, then in the height of their first renown. Bentham was stirred to indignation by the tone of comfortable optimism that pervaded Blackstone's classical treatise. He denounced Blackstone as an enemy of reform whose sophistry was so perverse as to be almost a crime, an official defender of abuses with a "sinister bias of the affections." It does not now concern us to adjust the merits of the controversy as between Blackstone and his critics. It should be remembered, however, that while much of Bentham's animadversion is captious and unfair in detail, he was quite right in attacking the people who maintained that English law as it stood in 1776 was the perfection of reason, and in taking Blackstone as their best representative. And to Blackstone's merits as an

expounder he does full justice, declaring that "he it is
who, first of all institutional writers, has taught jurisprudence to speak the language of the scholar and the
gentleman." But we must pass on to Bentham's own
doctrine.

The foundation of the modern English theory of the
State is laid in Bentham's definition of political society.
"When a number of persons (whom we may style subjects) are supposed to be in the habit of paying
obedience to a person, or an assemblage of persons, of
a known and certain description (whom we may call
governor or governors), such persons altogether (subjects and governors) are said to be in a state of political
society."[1] It is worth noting, in the light of Sir H.
Maine's later criticism, that Bentham explicitly admits
the difficulty there may be in deciding whether in a
particular society a known and certain governor is
habitually obeyed, and consequently whether the society
should be reckoned political or natural; a natural
society being defined as one where this habitual
obedience does not exist. He is quite aware that there
is in the facts of human society nothing corresponding
to the definition with perfect accuracy. "Few, in fact.
if any, are the instances of this habit being perfectly
absent, certainly none at all of its being perfectly
present." Practically the mark of a political society

---

[1] I spare the reader Bentham's profuse italics and capitals. Does
his "supposed" mean "understood in fact"? or does it mean or
include being required by law? Sovereignty, as formal authority to
issue rules not amendable by any higher authority—the plenary power
of legislation—is matter of law; habitual obedience is matter of fact.

is " the establishment of names of office," the existence
of people set apart for the business of governing and
issuing commands.

Laws are the commands of the supreme governor, or,
to use the term now adopted, the sovereign. And the
field of the supreme governor's authority is indefinite.
In practice, indeed, it is limited by the possibility of
resistance, and there are conditions under which
resistance is morally justifiable or proper. But these
conditions are not capable of general or precise definition. For the purpose of scientific analysis the power
of the sovereign must be treated as unlimited. The
difference between free and despotic governments is
in the constitution of the sovereign authority, not in
its power; in the securities for the responsibility of the
particular persons who exercise it, and for free criticism
of the manner of its exercise, not in any nominal
restriction of its scope. To say that a supreme
legislature cannot do this or that, or that any act of
such a body is illegal, is an abuse of language. " Why
cannot? What is there that should hinder them?"
Those who profess to discuss the power of the sovereign
are really discussing, in a confused and obscure way,
whether the acts of that power are useful or mischievous;
in the last resort, whether they are so mischievous that
resistance appears better than submission.

Bentham admits, however, that there is no reason
in the nature of things why the authority of a sovereign
body should not be " limited by express convention,'
though he regards this case as exceptional and seems

to be thinking only of the relations between federated
States or between a protecting and a protected or semi-
sovereign State. If such a limitation is defined, there
is no difficulty in conceiving it; whether it shall be
imposed in any given case is a question of expediency.
Thus Bentham has some notion of what Lord Bryce
and Prof. Dicey have in our time named a rigid constitution; and he further suggests the possibility of a
regular machinery for constitutional amendment: and
this eleven years before the Constitution of the United
States was adopted. He clearly dissents from the
Hobbist dogma (whether he knew it in Hobbes or not)
that sovereignty is illimitable and indivisible.[1] Where
the ultimate supremacy may be in a federal government, or whether we are bound to say that it is anywhere, Bentham does not stop to inquire.

Again, he distinguishes between the legal duty of
obedience (the supreme power itself being supposed
unchallenged) and the political doctrine of non-resist-
ance. The sovereign prince or assembly governs without any assigned superior or formal check, but always
at the peril of being in fact overthrown, if it appears to
a competent number of the subjects that the evils of
submission are greater than those of resistance. Here

---

[1] "To say . . . that not even by convention can any limitation be
made to the power of that body in a state which in other respects is
supreme, would be saying, I take it, rather too much : it would be saying that there is no such thing as government in the German Empire ;
nor in the Dutch Provinces ; nor in the Swiss Cantons : nor was of
old in the Achæan league" (c. iv. s. 34). European federal systems, as
known in the eighteenth century, were very loose as compared with
those which have succeeded them.

too Bentham and Hobbes part company.   Hobbes,
if called on to state his real position in Bentham's
language, would no doubt have said that the evils of
resistance are always greater; but Bentham would
have declined either to accept this as evident, or to
accept Hobbes's forcible description of the miseries of
a state of war as amounting to proof.   In short, to be
legally supreme governor is one thing, and to govern
as you please is another.   Political duty is one thing,
moral duty is another.   In the political sense (which
at the present time we rather call legal) supreme
governors cannot have any duties.   Bentham is particularly severe on Blackstone for speaking of the duty
of the sovereign to make laws.

Yet we may say in another sense that the duty of
the sovereign to make laws is Bentham's capital discovery in political science.   For Bentham has, besides
and beyond the formal theory of sovereignty, a decided
and confident theory as to the purpose for which governments exist.   They exist for the common advantage of
the governed; or, in terms which to Bentham appeared
more accurate, in order to promote the greatest happiness of the greatest number.   Only one standard can be
found by which their acts can be judged, that of general
utility.   Here Bentham found the rule both of private
morals and of public expedience; and the practical
inference from combining this with his theory of
sovereignty is that the State has no excuse for being
backward in well-doing.   The greatest happiness is the
end of human action; abuses and grievances exist; let

then the supremacy of the State, the most powerful
form of human action, be set to work to abolish them.
Let the machinery of government and justice be simpli-
fied; let irrational and anomalous rules be swept away;
let the motives of abuse and corruption be removed, and
political duties made plain and easy of comprehension.
Let there be no superstition about old rules being
inviolable merely because they are old. Let no prescriptive privilege stand in the way of the general-good.
Above all, let none pretend a want of power to do these
things. The State bears not sovereignty in vain.
Non est potestas super terram quae comparetur ei, says
Hobbes : therefore fear the sovereign and obey. True,
says Bentham, obedience is good; but while I "obey
punctually" I will "censure freely." What is sovereignty
for, if it is not to be directed by every light of reason
towards the attainment of the common happiness?
The formula of the greatest happiness is made a
hook to put in the nostrils of Leviathan, that he
may be tamed and harnessed to the chariot of
utility. Indeed, if Leviathan will haul the chariot, it
matters little whether he has one head or many.
Bentham was equally willing to be legislator in
ordinary to the United States, the French Republic,
and the Emperor of Russia. Such is the connexion
between Bentham's theory of the State and his theory
of legislation. Taken together, they give us the ideal
of modern legislation, in which the State is active, not
merely in providing remedies for new mischiefs, but in
the systematic reform and improvement of its own

institutions. Down to the eighteenth century legislation was considered as an exceptional instrument of policy, and in England at all events regarded with a certain jealousy. The mysterious authority of custom which to this day rules the Eastern world was still in the air of Europe. The change which has come over the spirit and methods of law-making in the last few generations is almost entirely due to Bentham.

We have nothing to do here with the ethical value of Bentham's doctrine. It is enough to say that it had to be seriously modified even by his immediate followers. But there is no doubt of its power in the political field. Had it been more subtle, it might have been less successful. It had exactly that amount of generality and apparent reasonableness which even in England will make speculative conceptions operative in practice. Everybody thinks he knows what happiness means; and for practical purposes, indeed, it matters little whether it is precisely known or not. A public judgment of happiness, expediency, well-being, or whatever else we call it, is in the nature of human affairs a rough thing at best; and there is plenty of work to be done which ought to be done on any possible view of the nature of duty. The main point was to rouse the State to consciousness of its power and its proper business; and by persistent and confident iteration Bentham did this effectually.

We cannot, again, say anything here either of the many actual reforms which may be traced to Bentham,

or, on the other hand, of that part of his proposals, by
no means an inconsiderable one, which was hopelessly
out of relation to the feelings and habits of mankind.
There is an extraordinary mixture in his work of
practical good sense on some topics with impracticable
extravagance and obstinacy in others.[1]   But there is no
leisure to discuss this, nor would there be much profit.
Bentham's eccentricities have passed away harmlessly,
save so far as they prejudiced the reception of his really
valuable ideas.   It remained to complete the separation
of the theory of political sovereignty from that of the
ethical and historical foundations of political society.
This was done by John Austin, who finally cleared the
way, with labour which now seems uncouth and exces-
sive,[2] to the conception of a pure science of positive law.
The worker in this field assumes the sovereign authority of the State as for his purposes the ultimate source
of laws and legal institutions as they exist, and he
analyses and classifies them without regard to the moral,

[1] Bentham's want of touch of public feeling and its tendencies comes
out in startling ways in his doctrine of penalties.   Utilitarianism is,
in common understanding, associated with rational philanthropy, and
justly so on the whole.   Yet Bentham seems at one time to have
thought it practicable and rather desirable to burn incendiaries alive,
and several of his other suggestions are both cruel and otherwise absurd.

[2] Austin's manner is so repulsive (as even his admirers allow)
that it is hard to be quite just to his matter.   There is no injustice,
however, in saying that Austin's lectures are at all events not a desirable text-book for novices in jurisprudence.   Perhaps the best general
criticism of his doctrine is Leslie Stephen's: *The English Utilitarians*,
vol. iii. ch. 5.   The shortest is Lord Melbourne's, which the curious
may find in the *Greville Memoirs*, iii. 138, *anno* 1834.   J. S. Mill's
essay is useful as an exposition in good English by an unquestioning
disciple.

social, or historical reasons which may have moved the sovereign to approve them. Now this requires a process of highly formal abstraction, and the abstraction cannot be maintained in its ideal purity when we come to dealing with even the simplest facts. This, however, is really the case with all scientific and philosophical abstractions. Another short consideration has, I think, been commonly overlooked. If, in order to frame a science of positive law, we are to take the contents of existing legal systems as given facts to be sorted out by some logical method, it really does not matter from what source they are given, except that we must verify their formal authenticity. Municipal law is the sum of the rules of conduct binding on members of a particular commonwealth as such. Talk of the command of the State, the imprint of the King's printers, an authorized report, or what you will, the material is just existing bodies of rules; and it is certainly not the sovereign authority in the State that can or will, in point of fact, tell us in any particular case what the rule is. Interpretation is not less important than enactment from a legal point of view; while experience shows that it is, oftener than not, equally stable. Committing oneself to any theory of origins beyond historical fact seems to be, for a lawyer, the very heresy of confusing politics and law which Austin exhorts him to avoid. Austin, however, did useful work in his own country and generation. If his manner had been less dogmatic, and I fear we must say pedantic, a great deal of misunderstanding might have been saved. As it was, he not only dogmatised overmuch in his own chosen field, but despised accurate knowledge even of the law as it existed, and absolutely ignored history.[1] Further criticism of the "analytical school" became indispensable, and was supplied by Sir Henry Maine[2] and Mr. Frederic Harrison.[3] More lately Professor Holland has exhibited the results of the English school in a form wholly freed from the old controversial encumbrances, and thereby freed also from the extreme insularity which has prevented our former English publicists from being appreciated by Continental thinkers; and Lord Bryce has discussed the nature of sovereignty with not only technical but historical and statesmanlike competence. His demonstration that the cases which Austin's ultra-Hobbist theory will fit are really exceptional has not been answered.[4]

British writers, in truth, were content for almost a century to generalise from their own constitution,

[1] Merely technical criticism is beyond the scope of this work. We are not therefore concerned with the perplexing questions why John Austin, being a member of the Equity Bar, discoursed of law and legal institutions like one imbued with the vulgar error found among laymen that their sole function is punishment; and why, having studied Roman law in Germany, he not only failed to learn its spirit, but made mistakes in the letter almost as gross as Blackstone's.

[2] *Early History of Institutions.*

[3] Articles in the *Fortnightly Review*, not reprinted: 1878-9, vol. 24, N. S. 475, 682; a third article in vol. 25 is on the historical method.

[4] *Studies in History and Jurisprudence*, Oxford 1901, vol. ii. Essay X.; cp. Essay III. on Flexible and Rigid Constitutions; and see Prof. Dicey, *Law of the Constitution*, and H. Sidgwick, *Elements of Politics*.

assuming the unlimited supremacy of Parliament to be a normal example of legislative power.   England was visited, in the second and third quarters of the nine-teenth century, by a combination of rising intellectual curiosity with grossly defective training; and this made it possible for authors who knew a little political philosophy to impose the shallowest of dogmas upon lawyers who knew none.   When we turn to the facts of the civilised world, we can hardly find a legislature with unlimited competence outside these islands. Least of all does any such power occur, where one might at first sight look for it, in despotic governments; for such government is hardly possible without con-trolling traditions which have all the force of law.   No one could ever have said of the Tsar or the Sultan that he "establisheth forms of religion "; a Christian Sultan, a Lutheran Tsar, would be more revolutionary than a Turkish or a Russian republic, and neither the Holy Synod[1] nor the Shaikh-ul-Islám acknowledges any superior in spiritual affairs.   Hobbes would no doubt have advised the Sultan that he was no true monarch until he got rid of the Shaikh-ul-Islám; but the Sultan might reply that the adventure of reducing two heads of the Faithful to one was like to be as much as his own head was worth.   In these cases there are elements which are not formally mutable at all; in the case of a "rigid" constitution there are institutions alterable only by a special process differing

[1] On the occasion of Tolstoy's death in November 1910, this body spoke with a voice which openly contradicted the Tsar's.

in a greater or less degree from that of current legislation. A "flexible" constitution, knowing no difference between ordinary reforms and extraordinary inno-
vation, is the only type which the universal formulas
of Hobbism will explain ; and, as we have said, there
are very few such. Thus the definition of sovereignty
as illimitable and indivisible breaks down even before
we come to the problems of federal government.
Bentham confessed and avoided these difficulties to
some extent. Austin and his followers have attempted
to dismiss them off-hand, but have signally failed.
In federal states they are driven to assign the title of
sovereign to an authority which may be active not
more than once or twice in a century, or else to con-
found sovereignty with the ultimate and unformed
political control of the people at large : a confusion
which it was the very purpose of the "analytical"
definition to avoid. It is true, as Maine [1] pointed out,
that the scope of legislative experiment and the importance of legislation have greatly increased and are
still increasing ; and it was by their foresight in this
respect that the utilitarians were justified. But it is
not at all true that formal limitations of legislative
power are out of date in federal or even unitary constitutions, or tend to be less important. It may be that
some readers of these lines, if not the writer, will live
to see such provisions in force at Westminster itself.

We may now see that the doctrine of sovereignty,
so far from closing discussion, opened up another field

---

[1] His criticism does not touch upon the objections above mentioned.

of search beyond the domain of positive law.   We have separated the actual existence and authority of government from the foundations and reasons of government. The voice of the sovereign is the command of the State, and the State acknowledges no superior.[1]   But the sovereign may be an artificial and composite body. Such is now the case in every civilised government in the world.   This raises a new distinction between formal and substantial, or if we substitute *legal* for Bentham's *political*, and set free the latter term for a new special use, we may say between legal and political sovereignty.   Where does the supreme power of a corporate or compound sovereign in practice reside?   Even in the simplest case of a single assembly, say the Athenian Demos, the whole assembly is formally sovereign, but practically the whole are not sovereign unless they are unanimous.   The power of the whole is exercised by a majority ; whoever wishes it exercised in a particular way must persuade a majority to think with him, and if he can do this it is enough. What then of him who persuades the majority, Pericles for example ?   Is he sovereign too ?   Or if Aspasia persuades Pericles?   Is not this the vain and infinite search for causes of causes ?   The answer is plain.   Successful persuasion is not sovereignty.   Pericles persuades the majority of Athenian citizens, but that majority has no need to persuade any one : it commands.   And a

---

[1] This does not imply that the State need be an independent State for international purposes.   Here is another Austinian confusion. But this brief warning must suffice.

majority one way or the other will always be found.
We may conceive, indeed, though not believe, that a
sovereign assembly should be equally divided, and there
should be nobody with authority to give a casting vote.
In this practically impossible case the form of sovereignty
would be unimpaired, but the State would be at a dead-
lock. From this we may proceed to imagine the more
complex cases of assemblies voting not collectively, but
by sections or estates; of several bodies meeting and
deliberating separately, but acting only by the concur-
rent decision of all; and finally to apply these ideas to
the peculiar system of the British Constitution, which
appears to us by long habit familiar and natural, and has
been copied, with variations partly designed and partly
undesigned, all over the world. We have seen what confusion arose among the earlier publicists from unwilling-
ness to carry out the separation of politics from ethics.
A similar confusion long prevailed in the thought of
British publicists (not excluding those of the modern
utilitarian school), because they could not or would not
distinguish legal supremacy from the practical power of
guiding its exercise. Parliament is the supreme power
in England, or, in our technical terms, is the sovereign.
Everybody since Hobbes, who vainly strove to deny it
(though even he admitted a corporate sovereign to be
theoretically possible), has admitted and asserted so
much. But what is Parliament? Who is the wielder
of sovereign power? Let us open the last volume of
statutes. "Be it enacted by the King's most excellent
Majesty, by and with the advice and consent of the

Lords Spiritual and Temporal, and Commons, in this present Parliament assembled, and by the authority of the same, as follows." Here are, to all appearance, three distinct powers ; they might have been, and as a matter of history were near being, four. It is part of the positive law of the land, the law by which courts of justice are governed, that to make a new law they must all agree. The Crown cannot legislate without the estates of the realm, nor with one House of Parliament against the other, nor can the Houses of Parliament jointly or severally legislate without the Crown. But what is to make them agree ? What security is there that they shall not constantly disagree ? Why do Englishmen go about their business in confidence that this complicated machine, with apparently independent parts, will work smoothly and all together ? As far as the purely legal constitution goes, it is like a clock with three distinct sets of works for the hour and minute hands and the striking part, and no provision for their keeping the same time. The publicists of the eighteenth century were content to say, in effect, that the component parts of Parliament were really independent, and (to use the language of their own time) in a state of nature with regard to one another. The risk of a dead-lock, so far from being unreal, was regarded as the peculiar virtue of the British Constitution, and as exercising a moderating influence on all parties. It was argued with great ingenuity that the powers of King, Lords, and Commons were not only different in kind, but that they had been kept apart by the wisdom of our ancestors because the

conjunction of them in the hands of any one man or
assembly would be fatal to liberty. De Lolme, working
on lines similar to those of Blackstone, whom he often
cites,[1] proved that the balance could not subsist if the
executive power were not one, or the legislative were
not divided. The doctrine of sovereignty, even in its
barely legal aspect, is a complete solvent of this theory.
No one who has assimilated Hobbes can go on believing in the balance of constitutional powers. It has been
shown by Bagehot (as thinking people must have felt
before his time, but did not plainly say) that the British
Constitution in its modern form gives the practical
sovereignty to the majority of the House of Commons
and gives it in a most effectual manner. The machine
works as well as it does, not because the powers are
balanced, but because in the last resort there is only one
power.[2] The ultimate unity of sovereignty is disguised
by the very means which secure it; for those means do
not appear at all on the legal face of our institutions.
Government is carried on by a system of understandings
which for the most part have never been authentically
defined, much less acquired the force of positive law.
The study of these informal conventions, as distinct from

[1] He first published his work in 1771, and dedicated the revised
English edition to George III. in 1784.

[2] The foregoing sentences are purposely left as they were written.
Bagehot could not anticipate the crisis of 1909-1910. The two Houses
of Parliament having failed to agree in their interpretation of the constitutional conventions, a new kind of problem was raised. The Parliament Act, 1911, does not purport to be a final solution, but in my
opinion (which not all competent persons would agree with) is accept
able as a provisional restoration, with the unavoidable drawbacks
incident to statutory definition, of the doctrine generally held in the
latter nineteenth century.

the positive constitutional law which in the United States and in most Continental countries is to be found in some one solemn act of state, and in our country in such statutes as Magna Carta, the Bill of Rights, and the Act of Settlement, is really a new branch of political science.

No attempt will be made here to follow the course of political speculation on the Continent of Europe in the nineteenth century. There, for better or worse, professed philosophers have had a greater share of it than in these islands, and the publicist is apt to talk the language of metaphysics, whereas here, even if he happens to be a philosopher,. he tries to make himself understood by men of ordinary intelligence. Hence it is not possible to discuss Continental theories of the State in a moderate compass without assuming a certain knowledge of the general history of philosophy. The separation of politics from ethics (including the ultimate metaphysical foundations of ethics), of which we spoke above, is not only not effected, but in many Continental schools would have been very lately regarded as impracticable ; in some it would still be so. But it may be useful to point out why the English utilitarians always remained outside the main stream Down to the time when the remnant of them was swept, some willing and others unwilling, into the flood-tide of Evolutionism,[1] they supposed themselves to be

[1] Not Darwinism : and this not merely because Herbert Spencer claimed, and justly, to have been an evolutionist and made extensive applications of that way of thinking before Darwin declared himself, but because the corresponding movement in moral and political science was independent and earlier.

maintaining the teaching of experience against the whole brood of dogmatists. Troubling themselves little, as our insular manner has been since the Reformation, with what foreigners were about, and being concerned to wake English political and legal thought from a particular kind of dogmatic slumber, they quite honestly thought they had nothing in common with the "monkish" ages and the fancies of the Schoolmen. Bentham cheerfully dismissed "the pretended Law of Nature" as "nothing but a phrase,"[1] which a simple application of reason would explode. Little did he or his followers suspect that his touchstone of the greatest happiness had been used, four centuries before, by his brilliant countryman, William of Ockham, under the name of *communis utilitas* and in the very name of the Law of Nature. Still less did he remember, if indeed he ever read, that the principle of Reason or Reasonableness which runs through the whole of our Common Law, wherever technicality leaves it room, is just an English version of the Law of Nature. Least of all could the denouncer of "judge-made law" (an aberration disclaimed by all his followers) guess that in the fourteenth century one English judge had passed the censure in jest, and another rebuked him. "*Hillary*. Law is what the Justices will. *Stonore*. No; Law is reason."[2] And if he had been told that the Law of Nature—that is, the doctrine of man's duties as a moral and social being, so far as discover-

---

[1] *Fragment*, c. iv. ss. 18, 19.
[2] Y. B. 18-19 Ed. III. (Rolls ed. 1905) p. 379.

able by natural reason alone—had been a rationalising and liberal influence throughout the Middle Ages and even in the Renaissance controversies,[1] he would probably not have believed it.   In English thought, even now, Bentham's ethical theory is often opposed to those of modern Continental philosophers or an English adherent, such as Coleridge, as a system founded on experience and not derived from transcendental ideas; and it is assumed that the like opposition holds between the respective political theories.   In truth, Bentham's principle of utility is no whit less dogmatic than Kant's principle of the Practical Reason.   Whatever validity either of them has depends on its correctness as an interpretation of human experience, and they both appeal to experience to justify them.   In the political application it is abundantly clear that Bentham is as much a dogmatist as any propounder of natural law, in any of its varieties, or in the particular modern variety which may be described as theory of legislation based on philosophy of ethics.   He assigns a final cause to the State by abstract considerations of human motives in general, such as they appear to him, and without taking the slightest trouble to consult history or specific facts, and he constructs a universal theory of legislation accordingly.

[1] After being used against the extreme claims of the Roman See, it was used by Romanists against the extreme letter-worship of Protestant controversialists.   Accordingly some Protestant writers expressly, and contrary to the scholastic tradition, declared the Law of Nature to be inferior in authority to the Law of God, by which last they meant the text of the scriptures interpreted in their own sense without regard to tradition.

His construction is of pattern institutions and rules
of law not limited in terms or intention to the circumstances of England or any other particular country.
His chapter on " Title by Succession " in *Principles of
the Civil Code* is as much *Naturrecht* as anything one
can find in Germany, for it lays down rules purporting
to be justified by the universal nature of human
relations, and qualified by no respect of time or place.
Such is not the positive law which lawyers discuss and
administer at Leipzig or Paris any more than in
London.[1]   An English lawyer may come upon a bit of
land in one parish which descends to all the tenant's sons
equally, and a bit in the next parish which descends to
the youngest son alone.   It concerns him not for the
matter in hand which rule looks more like an expression
of the rational will of the community, or better fitted
to promote the greatest happiness.   Each rule will be
enforced as to the land subject to it, and without discussion of its being reasonable or otherwise, and his
client's title will depend on the correct ascertainment
and application of the rule as it exists.   Again, if there
is any work of political reasoning which belongs purely
and simply to the English school, it is the collection of
notes appended to the first draft of the Indian Penal
Code, a most interesting and instructive document
which for many years has been accessible to English
readers in Lady Trevelyan's edition of Lord Macaulay's

[1] German critics having both a philosophical and a legal outlook,
Brunner and Kohler, have perceived this, and dismiss the utilitarians,
none too civilly, as a mere belated variety of natural-right theorists,
or *Naturrechtler*, incapable of profiting by history.

works.[1]   But the substance of these notes, except so far as they relate to provisions specially adapted to the circumstances of British India, and except so far as the framers of the Code may have been influenced, without knowing it, by any peculiarities of English positive law, is no less pure and simple *Naturrecht*.

Still there is a certain mutual repulsion between English and Continental speculation in this field. We must not say British, for Scotland goes, on the whole, with the Continent. What is the explanation of this ? The German or Germanising philosopher is ready with an easy one. " It just means," he would say, " that you English have not taken the pains to understand modern philosophy. You are still in the darkness of the præ-Kantian epoch, and you will never get a real theory of the State or of law till you come out of it. When you show signs of doing that, we may attend to what you have to say." There are Englishmen on the other hand who would be no less ready with their answer. " We confess," they would say, " that we know very little of your transcendental philosophies, and care less. It appears to us that you get nothing out of them but interminable vague talk about *Persönlichkeit* and *Menschenwürde*, or *le bien* and *l'idéal*, as the case may be, and that when it comes to distinct questions of policy you have to deal with them really by the same empirical methods as we do, and in much more cumbrous language." In each of

[1] It has been largely and properly used by the commentators on the Penal Code ; but it should be read as a whole.

these charges there is both truth and exagger-
ation. Continental critics ignore the English school
because they suppose it to be tied down to Bentham's
form of utilitarianism, whereas the true character of
English political science is to be found in the series of
distinctions by which our publicists have assigned
separate fields to political ethics, constitutional politics,
and positive law. The process was begun by Hobbes
and virtually completed by Hume. Hobbes began it
unconsciously by trying to make legal supremacy the
final and conclusive standard of political ethics. The
Whigs, with Locke's aid, strove to restore the ethical
element by working the law of nature, through the
machinery of the original contract, into the technical
conception of political supremacy itself. The original
contract was slain by Hume and trampled upon by
Burke, and the separation of the ethical part of politics,
as the theory of legislation and government, from the
analytical part, as the theory of the State and of positive law, was forced upon Bentham and his successors.
The theory of legislation must to some extent involve
a theory of ethics, though it need not involve any
decision upon ultimate metaphysical questions. But
the analytical branch of political science, including
the pure science of positive laws, is altogether independent of ethical theories, though not of the fact
that in every commonwealth there are received moral
standards which the rules of law must in the long run
follow. And that is the definite scientific result
which we in England say that the work of the past

century has given us. The precision and abstraction
which we have succeeded in attaching to our technical
terms was mistaken, until quite lately, by foreign
students, and even by able Scottish followers of the
Continental methods like Lorimer of Edinburgh, for
crudeness and narrowness of thought.

The English student, in turn, is naturally repelled
by this misunderstanding, and is prone to assume that
no solid good is to be expected of philosophers who
have not yet clearly separated in their minds the notion
of things as they are from that of things as they ought
to be. The German school seems to him to mix up
the analytical with the practical aspect of politics, and
politics in general with ethics, in a bewildering manner
But he must not assume that we and the Germans are
talking about the same things when we use corresponding terms, or even an Englishman and a Scotsman
when they use the same terms. He must allow for
the necessary difference in point of view between those
who have the two words *law* and *right*, and those for
whom *Recht* or *droit* covers both, so that our " law "
and " right " (even when " right " means the particular
right of an individual) appear as aspects of one and
the same thing, " Recht im objectiven Sinne " and
" Recht in subjectiver Hinsicht." Probably the
Germans think this a difference to their advantage.
We do not; but the difference must be remembered
in any case. When we take the thing as we find it,
not expecting it to be something else, we shall discover
this mysterious and terrible *Naturrecht* to be no worse

than a theory of government and legislation quite
legitimately descended from the old law of nature;[1]
or, to preserve better the wide generality given to it
by its authors, a kind of teleology of the State and
its institutions, differing much, indeed, from anything
of the kind in English literature, and as much involved
with ethical philosophy of Kantian or post-Kantian
schools as Bentham's theory of legislation is involved
with his utilitarianism. But we shall make out, held
in solution in this unfamiliar vehicle, much subtle
discrimination and sound political thought. There is
no intrinsic reason why the two methods should not
come to a *modus vivendi*, or at least to intelligent and
useful criticism of one another.

The difference between the two points of view is
hardly to be attributed to any essential difference
between the English and the German mind, but rather
to the difference of historical conditions. In England
the positive law of the land has for centuries been
single, strong, and conspicuous in all public life, and
therefore positive law presented itself as an adequate
object for distinct scientific study. In Germany there
were down to our own time a great number of
independent States, many of them very small, and
each with its own local law, but all having their laws
framed more or less on the same sort of pattern, and
looking for authority, in the absence of specific

---

[1] This has to be remembered in considering Continental (and to some
extent American) treatment of the law of nations, which was raised
by Grotius from the same stock.

enactment or custom, to a common stock of Roman or Romanised German tradition. In this state of things it was impossible that theory should not busy itself with the common stock of ideas to the neglect of their multitudinous and varying applications in actual use. And it is significant that in the United States, where a number of independent municipal jurisdictions find their general source of authority in the common law, much as the German States found theirs in the Roman law, and share the common stock of English legal ideas, exactly the same thing has happened. In spite of English tradition and communications, the bent of modern American publicists has been rather towards the Continental habit of thought.

In fact, however, the chances of an understanding between the abstract political thinking of England and of Germany were spoilt by the advent of a wholly different school which dominated European studies in most of the moral sciences for half a century or more, the historical school eminently so called. J. S. Mill was perhaps the last considerable English writer on politics who ignored its importance. Publicists of this school seek an explanation of what institutions are, and are tending to be, more in the knowledge of what they have been and how they came to be what they are than in the analysis of them as they stand. Savigny, the greatest master of jurisprudence in modern times, is the chief representative of the historical school in Germany, though the application of the method to the general theory of politics fills but a small proportion of his admirable work. In England Burke is recognised by the Germans themselves as his forerunner, and Coleridge's political writings, which, though less practical, are similar in their spirit and influence, must be assigned to the same class. The general idea of the historical method may be summed up in the aphorism, now familiar enough, that institutions are not made, but grow. "The state does not exist for purposes of men, and is not governed by laws of their devising, but by the cosmic force above. . . . Laws are found, not made . . . the force preparing the future is the same that made the past."[1] Thus Savigny, instead of giving a formal definition of law, describes it as an aspect of the total common life of a nation; not something made by the nation as matter of choice or convention, but, like its manners and language, bound up with its existence, and indeed helping to make the nation what it is; so that (as we have already noted) he says, in almost the same words as Burke, that the people is always the true legislator : *Das Gesetz ist das Organ des Volksrechts*. Thus Coleridge, in his essay on Church and State, considers the Church of England not as he actually finds it, nor yet as somebody might wish the Church to be if he were devising an ideal commonwealth, but in what he calls its idea ; that is, what the English Church, from its place and conditions in the English commonwealth. seemed to him fitted to be, and but for disturbing causes might be.

[1] Lord Acton, "German Schools of History," *Eng. Hist. Rev.* i. 9, reprinted in *Historical Essays and Studies*, 1907 (which see for fuller account from the historian's point of view).

This method leads to a certain optimism which is its danger; not the rationalist optimism of the eighteenth century which makes out that whatever is is best, but a speculative optimism which tries to see that whatever is becoming, or is continuously in a way to be, is best. Exactly the same danger has beset the kindred doctrine of evolution in modern natural science, and we may call this the optimism of historical evolution. For the rest, the historical method is many-sided, and in England it has never been appropriated by any defined school. It is needless to dwell on the power with which Maine used it among ourselves to throw light on legal and political ideas. In the field of the English Constitution it has been excellently represented by Freeman. Cornewall Lewis's book on the *Methods of Observation and Reasoning in Politics* is another good English example of the method in a more general way. The reader is purposely left to supply later ones from his own studies. In the last forty years of the nineteenth century historical knowledge in every department was reinforced or rather transformed by the progress of archaeology and anthropology, by the adoption of more exacting standards of criticism, and above all by the comparative study of institutions. The work of Jhering, a man of genius not to be neatly classified, may be said to mark the transition: Amari of Palermo was a precursor who, falling on the evil times of Italy, and dying in 1870, was not known as he ought to have been. Among recent and living representatives of modern methods one may name Lord Acton, Maitland, Sir A. Lyall,

Salomon Reinach, Esmein, Brunner, Gierke, Redlich, Villari, President Lowell. The cult of original research may, no doubt, be exaggerated. A handful of new documents does not make a historian. Still the fault is on the right side.

Want of space must be the excuse for omitting to follow out or even indicate other modern developments of political speculation. It would be tempting to trace in the work of independent writers who were not professed historians or archaeologists, such as Bluntschli, Holtzendorff, Taine, Henry Sidgwick, the results of a philosophical temper combined with technical training and a wide command of historical knowledge; to endeavour to fix the place of Positivism among other recent theories, or to assign the relation to previous English thought of the system unfolded in our own day by Herbert Spencer, a much more important one in my opinion than Auguste Comte's. But not one of these topics could be dealt with to any good purpose in these few pages.

The utilitarians rather disliked the newer fashion of research so far as they knew anything of it; Maine got only perfunctory recognition at the hands of their remnant. Yet in another direction they were in line with a European movement of considerable importance. Benthamism was not individualist in the sense required by the figment of a Social Contract, which, as we have seen, Bentham repudiated. Still the formula, "the greatest happiness of the greatest number," taken word for word, regards the State as a numerical sum of its citizens, contrary to the opinion of all the deeper thinkers on politics from Plato and Aristotle downwards. Hence a presumption that the business of the State is only or mainly to prevent individuals from jostling one another beyond what is inevitable or tolerable ; and this, being encouraged by other and purely economic doctrines, produced the watchword " laissez faire," [1] so that in the result " legislative utilitarianism is nothing else than systematised individualism." [2] Further, this view was in harmony with the conception of sovereignty from which Bentham started. Law was regarded merely as the command of the supreme power, and exclusive attention to its restraining function caused legal compulsion to be regarded as in its nature evil; and it followed that there ought to be as little of it as was compatible with the preservation of society. Continental speculation on the limits of State action had an independent origin. The question how far the State ought to exercise general control over the private action of its citizens, whether severally or in association, was definitely stated in its modern form by Wilhelm von Humboldt in a little book written in 1791, but not published till after the writer's death, sixty years later. Meanwhile a good many things had happened. Among others,

[1] Some individualists have even attempted, by a curious perversion, to regard Free Trade as a mere branch of an assumed universal principle of non-interference. The nearest approach I know to a contrary formula is the familiar precept of the elder sister in *Punch* : "Go and see what baby's doing and tell him he mustn't."

[2] Dicey, *Law and Public Opinion*, 174. Cf. the whole section, pp. 145-209.

Wilhelm von Humboldt himself, who in this book had
proved that public instruction was one of the things the
State ought on no account to meddle with, had been the
Prussian Minister of Education.   I do not know that he
ever retracted his former opinion ; he had no occasion
to do so, not having published it; but deeds are more
eloquent than words in such a case.   His earlier essay
was, in fact, the most natural protest of an active mind
against the fussy paternal government of the little
German States in the latter half of the eighteenth
century.   No doubt it was expressed in general terms.
Equally general in terms was Locke's plea for the
Revolution of 1688.   How far Humboldt's arguments
remained applicable to Prussia or other German States
in 1851, it is not our business to inquire.   It seems,
however, a curious and at first sight a gratuitous proceeding to adopt them as at that time applicable to the
state of government and public opinion in England.
But we have a way of infelicitous borrowing from our
neighbours.   In metaphysics Sir William Hamilton had
some little time before invented, by a wonderful misunderstanding of Kant, the spectre called the Un-
conditioned, which was gravely taken by himself and
a few disciples for a hopeful foundation of systematic
philosophy.   Somewhat after the same fashion the
English publicist who was afterwards Hamilton's most
brilliant opponent was pleased to take up the cry of
the over - regulated Prussian, and the result was the
essay which we all know as *Mill on Liberty*.   The
same line was taken up by Eötvös in Hungary (as

Hungary was under Austrian repression), and M. Edouard Laboulaye in France, a few years later, summed up and adopted the arguments of all these writers; with what provocation, any one who knows even slightly what French administration was during the nineteenth century, and particularly during the Second Empire, may easily guess. Later Herbert Spencer followed on the same side (though he declared himself in his earliest work, *Social Statics*, some years before J. S. Mill's essay was published),[1] and was encountered by Huxley, who called the minimising doctrine by the ingenious name of "Administrative Nihilism."[2] This was not acceptable to Spencer, who proposed the more neutral but less striking term, "Specialised Administration." In "The Man *versus* the State" (1884) Spencer reasserted his opinion of the mischief of State interference. On one point, that of the regulation of railways, he forgot that railways owe their existence to wholesale interference with private ownership, and that their liability to special control (whether or not it be wisely exercised in the interest of the public) is only a price paid to the State for special privileges, and therefore at all events involves no essential injustice. Mill's particular exposition was vigorously criticised by the late Sir James Stephen

[1] He afterwards explained that *Social Statics* must not be taken as representing his matured opinions. In that work he even talked of a supposed "right of the individual to ignore the State." In the natural organism a member that attempts to ignore the body is taught its mistake swiftly and sharply enough.

[2] See his *Method and Results*.

in his book named *Liberty, Equality, Fraternity*, so
much entangled with transitory polemic that its real
merit is obscured in the eyes of a younger generation.
For some time past the controversy has run more
upon economical and social than upon political lines,
being mixed up with discussion of private property, co-
operation or profit-sharing as against compulsory distribution of capital, and other like matters which it is
beyond my purpose to deal with.   Socialism, so far as
the many different and even contradictory senses in
which that word is used have any common root, is the
political application of economic tenets and not a theory
of politics at all.   It has no necessary connexion with
any form of government.   A despotic monarchy or
theocracy may be socialist; a democracy may be anti-
socialist.

The only remark of my own I have to add is
this: that the minimisers appear not to distinguish
sufficiently the action of the State in general from
its centralised action.   There are many things which
the State cannot do in the way of central government, or not effectually, but which can be very well
done by the action of local governing bodies.   But
this is a question between the direct and the delegated activity of the State, not between State action
and individual enterprise.   It is just as much against
the pure principles of Humboldt and Herbert Spencer
for the Town Council of Birmingham or Glasgow to
regulate the gas and water supply of its own city as
it would be for the Board of Trade to regulate it.   It

is hardly needful to point out that, on the principles
of pure individualism, all national and public museums,
picture galleries, parks, and the like, must cease to be
provided for out of public resources, and the further
maintenance of such things, if they are to be maintained at all, must depend wholly on private munifi-
cence and voluntary contributions.

As to the question in its general bearing, I do not
think it can be fully dealt with except by going back
to the older question, " What does the State exist for ? "
And although I cannot here justify myself at length, I
will bear witness that for my own part I think this a
point at which we may well say, " Back to Aristotle."
The minimisers tell us that the State exists only for
protection.   Aristotle tells us that it was founded on
the need for protection, but exists for more than protection—γινομένη μὲν οὖν τοῦ ζῆιν ἕνεκεν, οὖσα δὲ
τοῦ εὖ ζῆιν.   Not only material security, but the perfection of human and social life, is what we aim at in
that organised co-operation of many men's lives and
works which is called the State.   I fail to see good
warrant of either reason or experience for limiting the
corporate activity of a nation by hard and fast rules.
We must fix the limit by self-protection, says Mill ;
by negative as opposed to positive regulation, says
Spencer.   But where does protection leave off and interference begin ?   If it is negative and proper regulation
to say a man shall be punished for building his house
in a city so that it falls into the street, why is it positive
and improper regulation to say that he shall so build

it, if he builds at all, as not to appear to competent
persons likely to fall into the street? It is purely
negative regulation, and may therefore be proper, to
punish a man for communicating an infectious disease
by neglect of common precautions. Why is it improper to compel those precautions, where the danger
is known to exist, without waiting for somebody
to be actually infected? Herbert Spencer would
have had the State protect both property and contracts. One or two zealous maintainers of his views
have outdone their master by arguing that the
State should protect only property in the strict sense,
and leave contracts to take care of themselves.[1]
Why stop there? Somebody else may say that law is
restraint, and restraint is force, and the State ought to
use its force only against actual force; in other words,
to protect persons directly, and property not otherwise
than indirectly through persons; from which it would
be but one step more to the triumphant establishment
of the perfect "liberty of the subject" in Hobbes's
state of nature, which is a state of universal war.
I prefer to say with Huxley, who was no dealer
in empty phrases, that government is the corporate
reason of the community; with Burke, philosopher
and statesman, that a State "is not a partnership
in things subservient only to the gross animal existence of a temporary and perishable nature," but "a

[1] Many vigorous individualists, however, are indignant at the least
appearance of disparaging the sanctity of contract: which would be
more intelligible if they believed in a Social Contract as the foundation
of the commonwealth.

partnership in all science, a partnership in all art, a partnership in every virtue, and in all perfection;" and with Hobbes, but in a higher and deeper sense than he enforced, *Non est super terram potestas quae comparetur ei.*

INDEX

(MAINLY OF PROPER NAMES)

Aquinas, St. Thomas, his book *De Regimine Principum*, 37
Aristotle, 1, 15 *sqq.*, 38, 54, 130
Austin, John, 109

Bentham, Jeremy, 101 *sqq.*
 his definition of political society, 103
 admitted conventional limitation of sovereignty, 104, 105
 his application of the principle of utility, 106
 much of his work is *Naturrecht*, 121
Blackstone, William, on origin of Society, 84
 whether influenced by Montesquieu, 89
 criticised by Bentham, 102
Bodin, Jean, 47
 his definition of sovereignty, 49-55
 his relation to Hobbes and Montesquieu, 55-56
Bracton, Henry of, 41
Bryce, James, 34, 51, 105, 111
Burke, Edmund, 89 *sqq.*, 123, 135

Cicero, M. Tullius, on the Commonwealth, 31
Coleridge, S. T., on Church and State, 127
Communism, Aristotle on, 22
Comte, Auguste, 129
Contract, original or social, in Locke, 72, 75
 in Rousseau, 80, 82

Contract, original or social, in Blackstone, 84
 Burke on, 94
 Contrat Social, Rousseau's, 79-80

Dante Alighieri, his *De Monarchia*, 37, 39
Darwin, Charles, 118
Defensor Pacis, 44
De Lolme, John Louis, 117
Dicey, Prof. A. V., 105, 111, 130
Divine right of kings, 69, 70

England, Montesquieu's remarks on, 88
Evolutionism, 118

Figgis, J. N., his *Divine Right of Kings*, 70
Fortescue, John, his work in English Constitutional Law, 56
Frederick II. (*stupor mundi*), 35
Freeman, E. A., 128

Government, classification of its forms, 13, 26
Gray, John C., 52

Hamilton, Sir William, 131
Harrison, Frederic, 111
Historical school in Europe, 126
Hobbes, Thomas, 20, 50, 58, 123, 136 *sqq.*
 his doctrine contrasted with Locke's, 73, 76-78
 his obligations to Bodin, 55, 56
Holland, Prof. T. E., his *Elements of Jurisprudence*, 67, 111

Hooker, Richard, 70
Humboldt, Wilhelm von, on limits of State regulation, 130
Hume, David, 85, 123
Huxley, T. H., 132, 135

Individualism, 130, 133, 135

Jhering, Rudolf von, 128

Kant, permanence of his work, 19

Laboulaye, Edouard, 132
Law, defined by Hobbes, 64-65
  by Rousseau, 80
  by Bentham, 104
  municipal, 110
  of nature, 119
  separation of from politics, 67, 85, 109, 123
Lewis, Sir Geo. Cornewall, 128
Locke, John, his Essay on Civil Government, 69 sqq.
Lorimer, James, 124

Macaulay, T. B., his notes to the Indian Penal Code, 121
Machiavelli, Niccolò, 43 sqq.
  his purpose in the Prince, 46
Maine, Sir Henry, 111, 128
Marsiglio of Padua, 42
Mézières, Philippe de, 43
Mill, J. S., on Liberty, 131, 132
Montesquieu, Charles de Secondat, Baron de, 86 sqq.
  his remarks on England, 88
  obligations to Bodin, 55-56
More, Sir Thomas, his Utopia, 57

Nature, law of, 119
Naturrecht, 119, 121
Newman, W. L., 30

Ockham, William of, 42, 43, 119

Parliament, "omnipotence" of, stated by Sir Thomas Smith, 58
  by Blackstone, 84
  political supremacy in, 117

Pericles, funeral oration of, 10
Plato, political theories of, 13, 130
Polybius on Roman constitution, 31
Presles, Raoul de, 43

Reasonableness, principle of, 119
Revolution of 1688, 77
Revolution, French, 83, 84, 96
Rights of Man, Declaration of, 3, 83
Rome, empire of, in mediæval theory, 39
Rousseau, Jean-Jacques, 20, 79 sqq.

Savigny, F. C. von, 127
Sciences, classification of, 4, 5
Selden, John, 79
Smith, Sir Thomas, his De Republica Anglorum, 58
Social Contract, 20, 30, 60, 79, 80
Socialism and forms of government, 133
Socrates, political theories of, 12
Songe du Verger, Le, 43
Sovereignty, Bentham on, 104, 105
  Bodin on, 49-55
  Bryce, James, on, 111
  Hobbes on, 62 sqq.
  Rousseau on, 80 sqq.
  Smith, Sir Thomas, on, 57
Sovereignty, divisible, 50
Spartans, character of, 11
Spencer, Herbert, cited, 27, 118, 129, 132, 133, 134
Spinoza, Benedict de, his Tractatus Politicus, 68
State, what is, 25
  limits of its intervention, 119 sqq.
Stephen, Sir J. F., 132, 133
Stoics, political ideas of, 30

United States, political speculation in, 126
  constitution of, relation to Sovereignty, 50
Utilitarians, their dogmatism, 120
  as individualists, 130

Vinea, Peter de, 36, 37

Printed by R. & R. Clark, Limited, Edinburgh.

BEACON PAPERBACKS

BP1   SCHWEITZER, ALBERT — An Anthology

BP2   GUTHRIE, W. K. C. — The Greeks and Their Gods

BP3   ARON, RAYMOND — The Century of Total War

BP4   FIEDLER, LESLIE — An End to Innocence

BP5   ORWELL, GEORGE — Homage to Catalonia

BP6   WOLFE, BERTRAM — Three Who Made a Revolution

BP7   CASSIRER, ERNST — The Philosophy of the Enlightenment

BP8   ROBINSON, C. E. — Hellas

BP9   BUBER, MARTIN — Between Man and Man

BP10   READ, HERBERT — English Prose Style

BP11   WEIL, SIMONE — The Need for Roots

BP12   HOOK, SIDNEY — The Hero in History

BP13   MUMFORD, LEWIS — The Human Prospect

BP14   BENDA, JULIEN — The Betrayal of the Intellectuals

BP15   HUIZINGA, JOHAN — Homo Ludens

BP16   HOFSTADTER, RICHARD — Social Darwinism in American Thought

BP17   HALEVY, ELIE — The Growth of Philosophic Radicalism

BP18   KOESTLER, ARTHUR — The Invisible Writing

BP19   FREUD, SIGMUND — Delusion and Dream

BP20   LUCAS, F. L. — Greek Poetry for Everyman

BP21   JAMESON, J. FRANKLIN — The American Revolution Considered as a Social Movement

BP22   BAINTON, ROLAND — The Reformation of the Sixteenth Century

BP23   BENTLEY, ERIC — The Dramatic Event

BP24   STARK, FREYA — Perseus in the Wind

BP25   BAGEHOT, WALTER — Physics and Politics

BP26   TARN, W. W. — Alexander the Great

BP27   ROSE, ARNOLD — The Negro in America

BP28   KIERKEGAARD, SOREN — Attack Upon "Christendom"

BP29   HALL, A. R. — The Scientific Revolution

BP30   MALRAUX, ANDRE — The Conquerors

BP31   BENTLEY, ERIC — What is Theatre?

BP32   TOYNBEE, ARNOLD — The Industrial Revolution

BP33   MAYORGA, MARGARET — Best Short Plays, 1955-1956

BP34   TRILLING, LIONEL — A Gathering of Fugitives

BP35   GANDHI, MOHANDAS K. — An Autobiography

BP36   STEIN, GERTRUDE — Lectures in America

BP37   SCHWEITZER, ALBERT — Indian Thought and its Development

BP38   MUMFORD, LEWIS — The Golden Day

BP39   BALDWIN, JAMES — Notes of a Native Son

BP40   CARR, E. H. — The New Society

BP41   WHITE, MORTON — Social Thought in America

BP42   BEVAN, EDWYN — Symbolism and Belief

BP43   DODDS, E. R. — The Greeks and the Irrational

BP44   LEWIS, WYNDHAM — Time and Western Man

BP45   POLANYI, KARL — The Great Transformation

BP46   SCOTT, R. F. — Scott's Last Expedition

BP47   SEIDENBERG, RODERICK — Post-Historic Man

BP48   DEWEY, JOHN — Reconstruction in Philosophy

BP49   HARNACK, ADOLF — Outlines of the History of Dogma

BP50   GIERKE, OTTO — Natural Law and the Theory of Society

BP51   BAUDELAIRE, CHARLES — The Intimate Journals of Charles Baudelaire

BP52 BENTLEY, ERIC — A Century of Hero-Worship
BP53 SPURGEON, CAROLINE — Shakespeare's Imagery
BP54 ALLEE, W. C. — The Social Life of Animals
BP55 BOYLE, KAY — Three Short Novels
BP56 SCHWEITZER, ALBERT — The Psychiatric Study of Jesus
BP57 IVINS, WILLIAM M., JR. — How Prints Look
BP58 NEHRU, JAWAHARLAL — Toward Freedom
BP59 BREUER, JOSEPH AND FREUD, SIGMUND — Studies in
Hysteria
BP60 GRUBE, G. M. A. — Plato's Thought
BP61 TROELTSCH, ERNST — Protestantism and Progress
BP62 BUTLER, E. M. — The Tyranny of Greece over Germany
BP63 BOORSTIN, DANIEL — The Mysterious Science of the Law
BP64 BUBER, MARTIN — Paths in Utopia
BP65 CANBY, HENRY S. — Thoreau
BP66 GASTER, THEODOR H. — The Oldest Stories in the World
BP67 GIERKE, OTTO — Political Theories of the Middle Age
BP68 HENDERSON, LAWRENCE J. — The Fitness of the
Environment
BP69 HERSKOVITS, MELVILLE — The Myth of the Negro Past
BP70 JOY, CHARLES R. — The Animal World of Albert
Schweitzer
BP71 SOHM, RUDOLF — Outlines of Church History
BP72 WHITEHEAD, A. N. — The Function of Reason
BP73 MAYORGA, MARGARET — The Best Short Plays, 20th
Anniversary Edition
BP74 FRANKEL, CHARLES — The Case for Modern Man
BP75 LOEWENBERG, BERT JAMES — Charles Darwin
BP76 GOOCH, G. P. — History and Historians in the Nine-
teenth Century
BP77 DE RUGGIERO, GUIDO — The History of European
Liberalism
BP78 RICHARDS, I. A. — How to Read a Page
BP79 BUCKMASTER, HENRIETTA — Let My People Go
BP80 SILVER, ABBA H. — Messianic Speculation in Israel
BP81 JONES, RUFUS M. — Spiritual Reformers in the 16th and
17th Centuries
BP82 COULTON, G. G. — Ten Medieval Studies
BP83 EGGLESTON, EDWARD — The Transit of Civilization
BP84 USHER, A. P. — A History of Mechanical Inventions
BP85 COULTON, G. G. — Inquisition and Liberty
BP86 VAN DOREN, MARK — Liberal Education
BP87 JOY, CHARLES — Music in the Life of Albert Schweitzer
BP88 MANSFIELD, KATHERINE — Novels and Novelists
BP89 MILLER, PERRY — Orthodoxy in Massachusetts, 1630-1650
BP90 STEIN, GERTRUDE — Picasso
BP91 HEINE, HEINRICH — Religion and Philosophy in
Germany
BP92 MAYORGA, MARGARET — The Best Short Plays, 1957-1958
BP93 RUSSELL, BERTRAND — Authority and the Individual
BP94 GLOVER, T. R. — The Conflict of Religions in the Early
Roman Empire
BP95 HAY, MALCOLM — Europe and the Jews
BP96 POLLARD, A. F. — Factors in Modern History
BP97 NICOLSON, HAROLD — Good Behaviour
BP98 POLLOCK, FREDERICK — History of the Science of Politics
BP99 FRIEDLÄNDER, MAX J. — On Art and Connoisseurship
BP100 MONNEROT, JULES — Sociology and Psychology of
Communism

DATE DUE

OC 31 '73			
OC 20 '74			
OC 14 '75			
MR 9 '82			
GAYLORD			PRINTED IN U.S.A.